MW00444685

HOW TO TEACH ENGLISH SPELLING

Other Books by John Fulford

The Complete Guide to English Spelling Rules

My 60 Job Resume

To Reach the Sea

Last Plane to Cochabamba

Hitchhiking to Serendip

HOW TO TEACH ENGLISH SPELLING

Including
The Spelling Rules and 151 Spelling Lists

By John J. Fulford B.Ed. M.A.

Author of **The Complete Guide to English Spelling Rules**

HOW TO TEACH ENGLISH SPELLING by John J. Fulford

Copyright © 2017 by John J. Fulford

Published by Astoria Press, Long Beach, CA

Author services provided by Kathleen Kaiser
www.kathleenkaiserandassociates.com

Publishing services provided by Pedernales Publishing, LLC
www.pedernalespublishing.com

Cover by Christine Di Natale
www.dinataledesign.com

Edited by Barbara Ardinger
www.barbaraardinger.com

All rights reserved. No part of this book may be used or reproduced in any form by any electronic or mechanical means (including photocopying, recording, or information storage and retrieval) whatsoever without permission in writing from the author, except in the case of brief quotations embodied in critical articles and reviews.

Library of Congress Control Number: 2017953054

ISBN Number: 978-0-9963799-2-2 Paperback Edition
978-0-9963799-3-9 Digital Edition

Printed in the United States of America

Contents

Preface

$\mathcal{S}$pelling is the unloved stepchild of the English language. Students hate to study it, teachers are frustrated when they teach it, parents are angry about it, and experts write long, useless articles about it. Inevitably, spelling is either scorned, ignored, or quietly pushed into the background whenever the subject of education is discussed.

But it is not possible to be fully educated without being able to read well. And it is not possible to read well without understanding English spelling. The ability to decipher and make sense of English spelling is the key to being able to read quickly and effortlessly and fully understand what is written.

In both the United States and the United Kingdom, roughly 85 percent of all children in juvenile detention are functionally illiterate. Most of them have either dropped out of school or will drop out. These children are not in prison because they are stupid or because they are psychopaths; they are there because they failed to learn to read.

Because they had serious difficulty reading the textbooks and other materials used in their classes, as well as the material the teacher wrote on the chalkboard, or printed signs and instructions on notice boards, they fell further and further behind, not only in English classes but also in most other subjects, with the result that they took no pleasure in school and saw no value in getting an education. Boredom and truancy inevitably followed.

Why should these two English-speaking countries have such a high rate of illiteracy? Also, why do native English-speaking students take years longer than other students to become literate in their mother tongue? Various experts have suggested a wide range of reasons, but the main reason is the extraordinarily convoluted spelling system used in English.

Despite the fact that English spelling is so important, the subject gets very little attention. Most of the hard work of teaching spelling is done in the lowest grades. As the students progresses through school, less and less time is devoted to spelling. By the time the student reaches high school, there is no formal teaching of spelling. Many students graduate from high school incapable of spelling even the simplest of words. Few, if any, colleges and universities offer remedial spelling courses, and thus many college students graduate with deplorable spelling skills. At the post-graduate level, there are scores of linguists busy studying every aspect of the English language - except spelling. It is not considered important enough for formal study.

When students enroll in teacher-training institutes, very few (if any) are given a spelling test. Of all the courses they have to take, none are devoted to the study of English spelling rules and the teaching of spelling. None of these students are given spelling tests before they graduate. The result is that too many teachers who have difficulty with spelling are sent out into the world to teach spelling along with English grammar and reading.

It is sad that English spelling has such a bad reputation. English is a fascinating, colorful, and extremely flexible language, mainly because of its extraordinary variety of words. Millions of people enjoy learning and studying unusual words, doing crossword puzzles, and playing word games like Scrabble. Many books have been written about the origins of words, and the words themselves can be seen as cultural artifacts that reflect history, geography, and our ever-changing way of life.

Teachers should always encourage any interest on the part of their students in the origin and history of English words. After all, your students are going to be using the language for the rest of their lives. Studying English word origins and history can also be a good opportunity to introduce some history and geography when you point out to your students that no other major language can claim to contain words borrowed from almost every other language under the sun.

Why I Wrote This Book

I wrote this book for two reasons. The first reason was because an extremely frustrated school principal asked me to write it.

He was frustrated because year after year his new teachers would arrive, keen and eager to get to work but with no idea how to teach spelling. They had passed all their courses and had their heads full of educational psychology and statistics and theory, and they knew their English literature, too. But when it came to teaching their students how to spell? They didn't even know where to start. It wasn't long before teaching spelling became a chore. The teachers went through the motions with little enthusiasm and with the result that students' spelling scores plummeted and reading ability followed.

The second reason is based on my own experience. I was educated in England, where my father was a journalist and my mother had taught English, and then I went to the University of British Columbia in Vancouver, Canada. My first teaching experience was in a one-room school in the far north. This school was in a village that consisted of a store, a service station, and half a dozen small houses. We had neither electricity nor running water. We also had a very limited stock of school supplies that had to last the school year. My 28 students lived in shacks and cabins scattered through the forest and would appear out of the winter darkness as if by magic every morning at 8 o'clock.

Teaching there was a wonderful experience. I had my problems and difficulties, of course, but everybody was very helpful and the cheerful enthusiasm of the children also helped smooth things out. Officially, my students ranged from one kindergartner to some sixth graders, but they were a mixed bunch with very mixed abilities and included three native Canadians and two French Canadians. For me, it was an extraordinary learning experience, and I learned more "on the job" than I had in many of my education classes at the university. It was there that I began to appreciate the problems with English spelling.

For my next school, I chose a junior high school in the center of British Columbia where the students were mostly Doukhobour. The Doukhobor are a Russian-speaking religious group who traditionally have little use for schools and education. The children turned out to be very friendly and eager to learn and, for me, it was an extremely interesting year. Although I didn't learn any Russian, I did end the year quite sympathetic to the Doukhobor, and equally sympathetic to their problems spelling English.

Next year, I moved back to Vancouver where I taught English and business law at the high school level and, eventually, decided to take a year out to teach in a language school in Barcelona, Spain. I thoroughly enjoyed my year in Barcelona and learned a lot about teaching English to foreigners. It was there that my interest in English spelling became more of an obsession than mere curiosity. Many of my students were university students polishing their English. They could speak and read English quite well but they refused to write much, claiming that looking up the spelling was a waste of time. English spelling, they told me, was an incomprehensible mess. Nothing I said seemed to convince them that there is a great deal of logic to English spelling and that there are rules that govern correct spelling.

Back in Canada, I taught high school English in Winnipeg and was soon offered a job as an ESL teacher at a night school. I taught two classes two nights a week to adult immigrants who desperately needed to learn English in order to get a job (and even a driving license). The students were from all parts of Europe and there was no textbook, so I had to use my imagination and come up with inventive ways using newspapers and anything else I could think of. I spent hours trying to explain English spelling. At the end of the year, the principal assured me that I had done a good job and tried to persuade me to stay on for another year. But it had been a bitterly hard winter in Winnipeg and the warm sun and blue skies of Southern California beckoned me.

In California, I married and switched to elementary teaching. My interest in English spelling had become a serious study by that time, and with my wife's help I began in-depth research, which included some university courses in linguistics and a careful study of the works of Noah Webster, plus great deal of time doing internet research.

Eventually, I put everything that I had learned into a book, The Complete Guide to English Spelling Rules. It was well received and quickly became extremely popular among teachers and home schooling parents, not only in North America, but in many foreign countries.

THE SPELLING RULES.

Many years ago, I reasoned that there must be rules that govern English spelling. The problem as I saw it was that few experts agreed that such rules even existed, so the rules were not taught to the teachers, who did not teach them to their students.

English is now the most widely used language in the world. Somewhere between 500 million and a billion people on every continent use it every day. There must be some form of general agreement how words are spelled; otherwise, there would be linguistic chaos. Over time, this general agreement has become a series of spelling rules. For historic reasons, the English language contains an extraordinary variety of words, many with strange letter combinations that can produce a bewildering range of sounds. Yet almost all of these words are subject to the spelling rules. There is a logical pattern to the spelling of most English words.

Notice that I said "most English words." There are exceptions to many of the spelling rules, but when we compare them to the number of words that do indeed follow the rules, the exceptions are surprisingly few. English spelling is a bit like chess. A student who tried to play chess without knowing the rules and knowing how each piece moves would be understandably frustrated. Our students are intelligent and curious. They want too know the "how" and the "why" of English spelling. They are eager to know the rules.

NOAH WEBSTER AND SYLLABIFICATION

For many generations, spelling was taught primarily by memorization. The student was given a list of words, and the teacher offered either a reward or punishment to persuade the student to memorize the words. Nobody thought to improve on this crude "carrot and stick" approach until late in the 18th century, when Noah Webster published his famous American Spelling Book (commonly called the Blue-Back Speller) in 1788.

Noah Webster was a practical man. He was a lawyer before he became a teacher, and he took an extremely logical approach to teaching spelling. He did not arrange the words in his dictionary in alphabetical order. He started with words of one syllable and gradually introduced longer and more complex words. He also broke all the words into syllables.

The words in Webster's Dictionary were divided into syllables because he had, quite logically, reasoned that when faced with any kind of complicated problem, we instinctively break it down into its component parts and study each part separately. This is probably why the Blue-Back Speller was so immensely popular. It sold more than sixty million copies over the many years it was in print, and the title "Webster's dictionary" turned into a generic term. Unabridged reprints of the 1824 edition of Webster's spelling book are still available, complete with the blue cover.

When Webster wrote in his introduction that "letters form syllables, syllables form words, and words form sentences," he was explaining that the sound formed by the syllable or syllables is the heart of any word. Each of these individual sounds consists of a vowel together with the consonants that give it a particular sound. There may also be two or more vowels making one sound; these are called diphthongs (pronounced *dif-thongs*).

Linguists have names like "morpheme" and "phoneme" for the various units of sound that make up syllables and words, but all your students need to know is that the separate and distinct sounds of P, E, and T, for example, when put together form a syllable: *pet*. That syllable can be a word by itself ("I *pet* the cat") or it can be joined to other syllables to form a different word ("car*pet*," "*pet*rify"). A good teacher will sound out any new word by emphasizing these individual sounds and syllables. It helps if the teacher sounds out each syllable slowly and clearly and repeats it a few times.

Today we take it for granted that this is the correct way to introduce a new word, but it was Noah Webster who first insisted on this approach. He had two very good reasons for doing so.

First, syllabication is the logical approach to learning how to spell. The student studies the bits and pieces that make up the word.

Second, an emphasis on pronouncing each syllable correctly is the best way to improve the student's diction. If the student pronounces the word correctly, he or she will have less trouble spelling the word.

It should be remembered that at the time that Noah Webster's first dictionary, A *Compendious Dictionary of the English Language*, appeared in 1806, North America and much of Europe were undergoing what is called the Industrial Revolution. North America was absorbing a flood of immigrants from all parts of Europe, many of them uneducated and most of them speaking another language. At the same time, the urban areas of England were also being flooded by poorly educated people from rural areas looking for work. In both North America and England, a common form of communication in English was essential. It might be impossible for all these people to speak alike, but at least they could all read alike.

Since Webster's time, there have been numerous serious studies that have proved beyond argument that breaking words down into their component syllables is the most logical and most productive method available for enabling students to learn how to spell English words.

HOW WE LEARN TO SPELL

I am quite confident that most teachers appreciate the value of syllabication and clear pronunciation, but we cannot avoid the hard fact that *correct spelling involves memorization.* Almost any other subject can be taught in a variety of ways, but learning how to spell English words invariably involves memorization.

There are two basic types of memory: short-term and long-term. Short-term memory is useful for shopping lists and finding the car keys and for students preparing for a test. For learning how to spell correctly, however, we need long-term memory.

When we consider long-term memory, we can compare the human brain to a modern computer. They both work the same way. When the eye sees a new word, the brain places it in a group with other similarly spelled words. The brain notes any similarity with these other words and also picks up and records a great deal of information from the context of the new word. Eventually, the new word is locked into this special group, and, whether we know it or not, we have learned a spelling rule that covers that group of words.

The brain is also doing a great deal of subconscious comparison with other words in its files. Any words that do not seem to fit will eventually become part of a subgroup or remain as anomalies. Since English is not a completely phonetic language, there will be dozens of word groups and subgroups, but the human brain can handle them as easily as a computer does. The only difference is that the computer is much faster and doesn't forget. But the human brain has one advantage over the computer: it can recognize and analyze new words that would only confuse the computer because the new words are not yet in its memory bank.

Needless to say, the more the student reads, the faster the process works. Every word the student reads, whether in a textbook or a comic book or an advertisement, is valuable input.

This marvelous computer that we call our brain is constantly at work sorting words into various groups by sound, by meaning, and by spelling. After months of reading, writing, and studying on the part of the student (or anyone else), the files will contain enough information to be able to formulate spelling rules that apply to the majority of words it encounters.

PHONICS OR THE WHOLE WORD?

Much has been written on the problem of teaching spelling, and numerous experts have produced various theories. The most vocal experts are the supporters of phonics. A French mathematician named Blaise Pascal introduced the concept of phonics in 1655, and the system has been popular ever since. Unfortunately, fewer than fifty percent of our words come from the Anglo-Saxon, which was a phonemic language. It's the other fifty percent that contain those strange and irritating spellings that confuse the student. Phonics is an important part of teaching reading and spelling, but it is not, and never can be, the whole solution.

Learning to spell words by recognizing the entire word—the whole word approach—was popularized by Horace Mann, an American politician with a keen interest in education and public schools. During the first half of the 19th century he supported the idea that entire words could be learned without the use of phonics. This idea was later supported by the famous linguist Noam Chomsky

In actual practice, we use both methods to learn to spell. With beginners, we start with phonics, concentrate on the sounds of individual letters, and use single-syllable words, gradually increasing the difficulty. Whenever a new word is introduced, we persuade the student to break it into syllables and sound it out. Eventually, the student will recognize the word and not need to sound it out. He or she may even anticipate some words because of the context of the sentence or the subject.

More literate students no longer need to sound out each individual word. They have reached the stage of word recognition and can read a sentence at a glance or scan a whole paragraph using context, syntax, and grammar as a guide to meaning. Very good readers can read a paragraph silently faster than they can speak it aloud.

Spelling lists

At this point, let me take a guess at how you learned to spell. You probably learned the way I learned and the way my father learned and perhaps even my grandfather: "Twenty words on Monday, and a spelling test on Friday."

There is nothing wrong with this method. It allows the teacher to keep a reasonably accurate record of the student's progress and have something concrete to show a parent. The weakness in this method lies in choosing those twenty words.

Many teachers just go along with the spelling book traditionally used in their school. They use the spelling list for that week, no matter what words it contains, and spend very little time explaining the spelling. This is the worst approach.

Other teachers are forced to use spelling lists that are either mandated by administrators or are part of a commercially-produced reading program. This program usually consists of a teacher's manual, textbooks, and supplemental material sold to a school or school district by a large publisher. They are popular with administrators because they usually include standardized tests which, in theory, can be used to map a student's progress. They are also visually attractive and extremely lucrative for the publisher. In those reading programs, however, spelling is often given short shrift. The emphasis is on reading, and no attention is paid to spelling rules. In fact, the authors of the programs rarely mention that spelling rules exist. When a chapter does include a spelling list, the words are usually based only on the reading assignment. They offer very little help for the student struggling with spelling.

Another popular approach is to choose words that the students are having difficulties with. While this sounds like a good idea, it tends to limit the students' vocabulary. If they stick with words they are familiar with, there will be little to no new word acquisition. Also, the students are probably having difficulty with a word because of its strange spelling. Unless the spelling is carefully explained, they will continue to have difficulty with that word.

When students have difficulty with a word, this is an excellent opportunity to introduce synonyms and antonyms. Finding another word that is similar, or opposite, in spelling or meaning is excellent for word acquisition. They will quickly learn the technical terms for such words. This is also an opportunity to introduce them to the thesaurus.

Another idea is to choose "useful" words, such as the days of the week, the months of the year, or the animals in the zoo. Such lists will have high student interest, but they will inevitably include words such as *Wednesday, February, knife-knives, rhinoceros, gnu,* and other words with strange spellings. With the limited time available for teaching spelling, the teacher is rarely able to carefully explain these words. The students are told to just memorize them.

Some teachers make up their own lists from other lists. Over the years, I have collected quite a few lists with titles like "The One hundred Most Commonly Misspelled Words" and "The Fifty Hardest Words to Spell." But they never state just how or by whom the list was made up, and few lists even agree with other lists. These lists always contain spellings that need to be carefully explained. If the words are commonly misspelled, there must be a reason.

So what words should we put in spelling lists? This will depend on the age and ability level of the students, but it is essential that, no matter the age of the students, whenever there is a spelling rule that governs that particular spelling, *the list should be based on a clear understanding of the rule.* Your students need to see a pattern to the words in the list, and they need to see the logic of that particular spelling. Only then will they remember how to spell the words.

The aim is to have every student earn a perfect score every Friday. If every student earns an A, this does not mean that the words were too easy. It means that they have remembered the spelling rule and applied it. The students will be happy with their progress, and the teacher will know that he or she has taught the basic rule successfully and that the students are beginning to recognize spelling patterns. To make sure that the students have fixed the words in their long term memories, they should then be asked to use the words in sentences and tested again some weeks later.

The chapters in this book are based on the spelling rules laid out in *The Complete Guide to English Spelling Rules.* It would be a good idea to have a copy of this book handy in case a particularly smart student asks a particularly awkward question, but I do not recommend that the students study only the rules. Each rule should be introduced along with the spelling words the teacher has chosen to exemplify that rule. For each chapter, therefore, I have included a sample of words that illustrate the rules. We can call these "word families." The teacher should choose from the list or add words as he or she sees fit.

Warnings!

(1) **Do not attempt to cover everything in just one school year. Choose carefully those elements that you believe your students can handle.**

(2) **Do not attempt to teach every word in the word lists. These lists are designed for all teaching levels and contain words ranging from simple, everyday words to words that even well educated adults often find challenging.**

To summarize...

The best way to teach English spelling is to teach the spelling rules reinforced by as many examples as necessary and to make sure that students break the words down into syllables.

But we have to be practical. Teachers simply do not have the time to research the spelling rules and then also research and create lists of words. In this book you will find both lists of words and the spelling rules that apply, plus anomalies and explanations. It's all ready to use.

If I have done it right, you should be able to make up a word list built on a spelling rule and adjusted to the age and skills of your students.

There are about one million words in the English language. This is more than any other language in the world and twice as many as any Romance or Germanic or Slavic language. However, because the average person has a vocabulary of about 20,000 words, I have chosen just those words that I consider commonly used and have kept to the minimum the scientific words, names, and exotic imports that organizers of spelling bees love to dig up.

How This Book Is Divided

This book is divided into three parts. Part One deals with the spelling markers, or guides, that control the pronunciation of many words.

Part Two deals with spelling problems that involve the use of consonants. Most students struggling with English have little difficulty with consonants, as they are generally predictable. So we tackle the easy part first in order to give the students confidence.

Part Three deals with spelling problems that involve vowels. It is the extraordinary variation of vowel sounds that causes most of the confusion in English spelling.

Naturally, every teacher or parent will choose where to start and what to study, depending on the ages and abilities of the students. You may want to start with the consonants or dive right into the vowel problem. Whatever you do, I believe you will be pleasantly surprised at how quickly your students learn and retain many of the spelling rules.

The Basics

$\mathcal{T}$eachers and parents should read this section carefully before explaining the basics of English spelling to their students.

When teaching very young or foreign students learning English, it is necessary to make sure that the students understand the basics. As the teacher, you need to know that they have a solid foundation.

THE VOWELS: A, E, I, O, U, AND SOMETIMES Y

Don't take anything for granted. First, make sure that the students understand that an English vowel can be short or long. **When teaching foreign students,** remember that many languages have only one sound for each vowel, and usually it is short. This is not true of English.

1. The short vowels are the sounds in these one-syllable words: *pat, pet, pit, pot, put, catch, fresh, sick, cloth, luck.*
2. Long vowels are the sounds in *made, feel, pine, home, cute.* These long vowels produce a wide variety of sounds, like *haul, hear, oil,* and *book.*
3. Two vowels together form a diphthong, which usually has a long vowel sound. There are over two dozen diphthongs. With diphthongs, the first of the two vowels usually controls the sound. For example, "He wore a *suit* and *coat* with a *plain cream tie.*" Always make sure that students know what a diphthong is and how to recognize one. The word comes from the Greek *di,* meaning "twice" and *phthongos,* meaning "voice or sound."
4. A digraph is also two letters together. Digraphs are usually consonants, but they can also be a consonant and a vowel. The word comes from the Greek *di,* meaning "twice" and *graph,* meaning "something written." Two consonants together are often called consonant digraphs or consonant blends. Examples are *ch, bl, tr, sw, sh,* and *th.*
5. *The letter Y is special. It should be considered another vowel because it is used as a vowel more than it is used as a consonant. As a vowel, it has three sounds, as in happy, shy, and the first syllable of gypsum.*

Half of English words are spelled the way they sound

About half of all commonly used words (the ones we read and write every day) are phonemic. That is, *they are spelled the way they sound and sound the way they are spelled.* It's the other fifty percent that confuse us. However, when we look closer, we will see that those weird spellings actually contain clues as to spelling and pronunciation.

Many languages use special marks called diacritics. These are the accent marks we commonly see in French words (*bête, théâtre, façade*), the Spanish tilde (*año* and *mañana*), and the German umlaut (*Das Mädchen ist dünn und schön*). Diacritics are rarely used in English, however, except with foreign words. Instead, we arrange the spelling to tell us how the word must be pronounced. For example, instead of the tilde, we use an I or a Y: *onion, canyon*. I and Y as used this way are called markers. There are about ten of these spelling markers that we use instead of diacritics, and there are spelling rules that explain how these markers are used.

SILENT LETTERS

English spelling has too many silent letters. Almost all the consonants are sometimes silent. Examples range from common words, like the B in *debt* and the S in *island* to more complex words, like the P in *psycho* and *pneumonia*, the N in *hymn*, and the first M in *mnemonic*.

Too many English words contain the old Germanic spellings like *ough* (as in *cough* and *through*) and *augh* (as in *laugh*) that should have been abandoned many years ago. These, along with *ph* instead of *F* (as in *photo* and *graph*), are serious stumbling blocks for many students. The only way to deal with them is to explain to the student that they are ancient and anachronistic and we hope that some future generation will get rid of them.

SYLLABICATION

First, explain to your students that a syllable is the sound made by a vowel or diphthong accompanied by the consonants that give it that sound. Examples: *cat, hen, pig, dog, duck*.

A syllable is not always a whole word. Prefixes and suffixes (together called affixes) are also syllables. Examples are *hap-py, hap-pi-est, un-hap-py, un-hap-pi-est*. *Happy* is the root word. *un* is the prefix and *est* is the suffix. Both affixes are syllables.

The spelling rules are as follows:

1. A closed syllable is a vowel followed by a consonant. These will be short vowels. They may be followed by two or more consonants and still retain the short vowel sound. Examples: *not, men, den-tist, pil-grim, vel-vet, o-poss-um*.
2. An open syllable occurs when the vowel is not followed by a consonant. In this case, the vowel will be long. The vowel in an open syllable is often called the *letter name*. Examples: *no, me, a-corn, be-ing, bro-ken, i-o-dine*.

Notes:

1. **When the letter Y is in a closed syllable, it should have the short I sound, as in** *hymn* **and the first syllable of** *gypsy*. **When it is in an open syllable, it will have the long E sound (the second syllable of** *gypsy*) **or the long I sound (***fry*, *ty-rant*).**

2. **When dividing words into syllables, never split a consonant blend or vowel diphthong. Examples:** *ill-ness, suck-ing, feel-ing*. **But double consonants are often split:** *em-bar-ras-sing, suc-cess, ac-ci-dent*.

Breaking a word into syllables is valuable because the student needs to know whether a vowel is long or short. Not only does this affect the sound and pronunciation of a word, it also almost always changes the meaning of the word. See the examples in the following list:

di-ning	*din-ner*
si-lent	*sil-ly*
de-feat	*def-er-ence*
o-pen	*op-er-ate*
ma-ting	*mat-ter*
ti-tan-ic	*tit-u-lar*
pro-pel	*prop-er*

Anomalies

There are a few cases where a vowel diphthong produces a short vowel sound. Examples: *head, dead, bread, thread, dealt, leather, health, sweat, dread, cough, rough, friend, plait.*

There are also a few cases where a closed syllable containing only one vowel does not produce a short vowel sound. Examples: *busy, monk, many, ton.*

Practicing syllabification for fun

Correct pronunciation is a very important aid to learning how to spell.

Just for fun, and to give the students practice, ask them to break this popular nonsense word (from *Mary Poppins*) into syllables: *supercalifragilisticexpialidocious.*

Su-per-cal-i-frag-i-lis-tic-ex-pi-al-i-do-cious

This next word was invented by Shakespeare, and he used it only once. It is the longest word in the English language that has alternating vowels and consonants. *honorificabilitudinitatibus.*

Hon-or-if-ic-ab-il-it-ud-in-it-at-i-bus

How to teach spelling.

When teaching the very youngest students in the primary grades (K to 3), use the phonic approach. Choose words from the list that have the short vowel, such as *cat, pet, sit, hot,* and *cut,* and make sure that the students understand the consonant sounds. When they are ready, introduce consonant digraphs such as *sh, ch, th, sp, bl,* and *d.* **Do not try to teach the spelling rules yet.**

As primary teachers have known for many generations, the phonic approach is the most logical for the very young. The children learn quickly and enjoy being able to read. But also remember that phonics is a trap! Those students who have grown up believing that all words can be sounded out easily and logically are the students who have the most difficulty with spelling when they are faced with words that cannot be sounded out easily and seem to be spelled in illogical ways. Therefore, the teacher must start including more difficult words as soon as the students appear to be ready for them. One guide is to listen to the children talking among themselves. Quite often, they will use sophisticated words in conversation. If they know and use such words, they are ready to learn how to spell them.

From my own years of teaching, I appreciate that your class time is limited and there are frequent interruptions. Your lessons don't always go as planned. This is why I have listed the points that have to be covered and the order in which to cover them.

Choose the words for the week and put them on the board. Have the students write them down.

It is not necessary to have exactly twenty words. (But it is a nice round figure for record keeping.) You choose how many words you think your students can handle. Just make sure that they all form a "family" of words that illustrate a rule.

Small children will print the words, but older students should write them in cursive. While the youngest children enjoy writing, the older students are not so enthusiastic. The main reason for this is that many of them cannot write. That is, they cannot write cursive. They print each letter slowly and individually in an ugly mixture of lower and uppercase letters. Cursive, sometimes called longhand or roundhand, was introduced during the 17th century to make it possible to write much faster than printing. Once your students have learned to write in cursive, they will not only be able to write twice as fast, but the finished results will look more attractive. You can make good cursive writing a source of pride for the students by always commenting favorably when you see a nice example.

Ask the class if they can see a pattern to the words. Then introduce the spelling rule and explain how it applies to the words.

When there are rules that apply to the words you have chosen, make the students write the rule. Just telling them is useless. "In one ear and out the other." Also make sure they have a copy of the list of words (and rules) to take home to study and to show their parents.

Break the words into syllables.

Pronounce each syllable slowly and carefully, then have the students repeat it. They should pronounce each syllable separately. Have the students tell you what the vowel or diphthong is and why it makes that particular sound. Discuss whether it is a long or short syllable. What are the clues to the sound? Here you may discuss the issue of regional accents. Everybody has an accent, but despite the fact that we each pronounce a word slightly differently from people in other cities or countries, we all spell the words and read them the same.

Play with the words.

This is a difficult but necessary part of word acquisition. What you do depends on the ability level of your students.

First, check to be sure they know what the words mean. Then ask your students if the words are nouns, verbs, adjectives, or other parts of speech. This gives you the opportunity to check that they all know what the parts of speech are. **Do not turn it into a grammar lesson.** Concentrate on the meaning and the spelling of the words under discussion. Your job is to get the students to see words as fascinating artifacts loaded with meaning that can be informative and flexible and extremely powerful when properly used.

Ask for opposites (antonyms) and similar words (synonyms). Experiment with adding suffixes or prefixes to the words. Discuss whether or not an affix works with some words but not with others. With verbs, study the tenses, especially the past tense, which often has a different spelling or form. Try to guess the root word, then look for words that appear to be from the same root. Introduce your students to Scrabble and crossword puzzles. Anything to get them interested in words. For the weaker students, one popular activity is to see how many words can be made from the word being studied.

If you have the time, read the famous poem "Jabberwocky" by Lewis Carroll, who wrote *Alice in Wonderland,* to them and have fun discussing the meaning of Carroll's strange words. Carroll called his made-up words "portmanteau" words, meaning they combined syllables and meaning of two different words. "Slithy," for example, means "lithe" and "slimy." Ask your students to identify other portmanteau words in "Jabberwocky."

Ask your students to write a short sentence that includes at least three of the spelling words. Ask for rhymes, short verses, or limericks. You may be surprised at their ingenuity.

Simply writing the words by themselves a number of times has very little value. It is better for the student to become familiar with the word in as many ways as possible. We learn to use tools by actually using them. We learn to spell words the same way: by becoming familiar with the words and using them often.

When giving the spelling test, pronounce each syllable carefully.

Take note of any word that seems to be a problem. Ask the students why they misspelled it. Analyze the problem and use that word in another, later test.

Part One: Markers

*E*nglish spelling contains markers, or clues, to the correct pronunciation. Markers warn us that the sound of the vowel has changed or that the sound of a consonant has changed.

1. Soft and Hard C.

This is a very common marker. Your students need to know when the C is going to be hard like K (*cat*) or soft like S (*cent*).

Spelling Rule. The C is soft when it is immediately followed by the vowels E, I, and Y. Examples: *cent, cinder, cylinder.* See List #1.

Spelling Rule. When adding a suffix that starts with A, O, U, or a consonant to a word that ends in CE, we usually retain the silent E so that the C does not become hard. Examples: *serviceable, noticeable.* See List #2.

Spelling Rule. When adding a suffix that begins with E, I, or Y to a word that ends in CE or GE, we **drop** the silent E, as it is not needed. Examples: *servicing, managing.* See List #3.

Spelling Rule. The C is hard when it is immediately followed by the vowels A, O, and U. Examples: *cat, corner, cucumber.* See List #4.

Spelling Rule. The C is hard when it is the final letter of a word or is followed by a consonant. Examples: *picnic, panic, climb, cry.* See List #4.

Spelling Rule. When adding a suffix that begins with E, I, or Y to a word that ends in a hard C, we must add K to keep the C hard. Examples: *picnicking, bivouacking.* See List #5.

Spelling Rule. When there are two C's together, the first will be hard and the second will be hard or soft, depending on the letter that follows it. Examples: *accident, accord.* See List #6.

LIST #1. Some words containing the soft C

CE	CE	CI	CY
cell	ace	city	cycle
cent	ice	cider	cyst
cedar	face	cigar	cynic
cease	dice	cinch	cynical
ceiling	lice	cist	cyanide
celery	mice	civic	cyborg
cellar	mace	civil	cyclic
cement	nice	cinder	cymbal
censer	once	cinema	cygnet
censor	brace	cipher	cylinder
center	dunce	circus	cypher
central	excel	cicada	cypress
cereal	fence	cigarette	cypress
censure	force	cistern	cyberspace
censored	grace	citadel	cyclone
century	juice	citrus	cylindrical
ceramic	laces	cilantro	Cyclops
certain	lance	cinnamon	cyan
certify	ocean	civilized	cybernetic
celibate	ounce	civilian	bouncy
celebrate	peace	circuitry	excellency
cemetery	biceps	circulate	spicy
centaur	cancel	cirrhosis	
caesarian	faucet	circumstances	
celluloid	glance		
centipede	grocer		

There are almost no exceptions to this rule except some scientific words like *coelacanth*, *coelom*, and *coelenteron*

Notes:

Cello is an Italian word and begins with the CH sound.

Arced is the past tense of *arc* and has the K sound.

Zinced, zincing behave the same as *arc.*

Celt is a Gaelic word pronounced *kelt.*

Mic is the short word for *microphone* and is pronounced *mike.*

LIST #2. Hard vowels A and O following CE and G retaining the E

CEA	GEA	GEO	CEO
serviceable	manageable	courageous	curvaceous
noticeable	salvageable	advantageous	cetaceous
enforceable	changeable	outrageous	crustaceous
replaceable	chargeable	umbrageous	siliceous
sliceable	bridgeable	rampageous	herbaceous
traceable	marriageable	gorgeous	
peaceable	forgeable		
danceable	enlargeable		
embraceable	exchangeable		
influenceable			

Note: The consonants L, M, and N following CE and GE retain the E:

CE	CE	GE	GE	CE
nicely	placement	engagement	hugeness	facileness
choicely	effacement	management	largeness	fierceness
fiercely	enticement	derangement	savageness	niceness
princely	defacement	arrangement	sageness	scarceness
scarcely	inducement	assuagement	strangeness	spruceness
sprucely	advancement	enlargement		conciseness
	enhancement			
	enforcement			

LIST #3. Some words that drop the silent E

CING	CIBLE	CY	SIBLE	GING
icing	producible	pricy	defensible	managing
dicing	forcible	icy	sensible	aging
juicing	coercible	lacy	infusible	edging
pricing	reducible	racy	reversible	paging
slicing	invincible	juicy	diffusible	raging
spicing	deducible	chancy	dispersible	waging
voicing		spacy		bulging
enticing		spicy		dodging
noticing		bouncy		
policing				
sluicing				
splicing				
invoicing				
rejoicing				
servicing				
practicing				
sacrificing				
dancing				
tracing				
placing				

LIST #4. Words containing the hard C

can	cot	cut
cat	cotton	cute
camp	cock	cubic
Canada	cold	cucumber
candy	content	cunning
click	clone	clumsy
cling	close	clue
crash	crop	crumbs
crazy	crown	crude
scalp	scrooge	scrub
scrape	scorch	scurry
cascade	discover	discuss
escape	disco	biscuit
epic	antic	attic
basic	magic	public
lilac	maniac	almanac
cuckoo	cushion	crumble
uncle	crush	cup
cuff	cub	crust
cling	clump	club
come	code	cone
cove	cope	coal
croak	coat	coast

Note: Show your students that the hard C can appear almost anywhere except before E, I, or Y.

LIST #5. Two-syllable and longer words ending in IC and AC

picnic	picnicker	almanac
traffic	trafficker	aphrodisiac
frolic	frolicked	insomniac
panic	panicked	cardiac
mosaic	mosaicked	maniac
plastic	plasticky	lilac
garlic	garlicky	amnesiac
		bivouac
		zodiac
		tarmac
		cognac
		sacroiliac

LIST #6. Words containing the double C

Note: The first column has one sound. The second column has two sounds, the K and the S.

The words in the first group will be difficult for your students, as most of these words do not really need that extra C, except as indicators that the preceding vowel is short.

accompany	accident
accomplish	success
accommodate	eccentric
accord	access
accordion	accept
account	accent
accrue	accelerate
accumulate	accede
accurate	vaccine
accuse	vaccinate
accustom	succinct
broccoli	accessories
hiccup	accentuate

List 6 Continued

occasion	accident
occupy	success
occupation	eccentric
occur	access
piccolo	accept
succulent	accelerate
succumb	accede
succor	
acclaim	
stucco	
occult	
tobacco	
raccoon	
occlude	
soccer	

Note: The word *soccer* was created in the late 19th century from "Association Football."

2. Combinations using C.

The letter C is a popular letter in English. It is commonly used in combination with other letters: CH, CK, CI, CE, and SC. These combinations often confuse the student.

Teachers: Do not try to teach this section unless you have a very advanced class. The information given here is mainly for teachers who will need it when students become confused.

When the C is followed by H, we usually expect the digraph sound produced by CH. Examples: *lunch, chip*. See List #7.

But the CH may have the SH sound. These are often French words like *cliché*. Also: *chute, machine*.

Sometimes the CH may have the K sound. These are often Greek words like *chorus* and *stomach*. See List #8.

When followed by K in one-syllable words with a short vowel, the C is silent, as in *sack* and *stick*. See List #9

When the SC digraph is followed by E or I, it has the SH sound, as in *crescendo* and *luscious*. See List #10.

After the letter S, the C is silent if it is followed by E or I. Examples are *scene* and *scent*. See List #9.

When the CI or CE digraph appears, it may have the SH sound, as in *ocean* and *atrocious*. See List #10.

Spelling Rule. The K has to be used instead of C when the K sound is needed before E or I. Examples: *kill, keeper, kennel*. See List #11.

No commonly used English word begins with CK.

LIST #7. Words using CH

chat	branch	change	batch
cheese	beach	chess	bench
china	flinch	chicken	rich
chop	porch	choose	crouch
chunk	lunch	chapter	chip
chocolate	chuckle		

LIST #8. CH with the K sound or the SH sound

CH with the K sound		CH with the SH sound	
mechanic	mechanism	machine	chiffon
ache	anchor	parachute	Chablis
archeology	architect	chalet	chassis
chameleon	architecture	champagne	chenille
bronchial	bronchitis	chandelier	cliché
chaos	chasm	charade	brochure
character	chemical	chauffeur	fuchsia
chemistry	cholesterol	chef	attaché
chorus	echo	crochet	cache
monarch	psychology	microfiche	chute
orchestra	orchid	mustache	choux
schedule	scheme	quiche	chivalrous
scholar	school		
schooner	stomach		
synchronize	lichen		
choir	alchemy		
archaic	dachshund		
arachnid	chorus		
chord	scheme (pronounced skeme)		
	schism (pronounced skism)		

Notes: These are the two main sounds of CH. The oddities are *cello* and the second C in *concerto*. These are Italian and have the CH sound.

Saccharin (sack-a-rin) is the only word in this group with double C.

The word *choir* (kwy-er) is a strange anomaly.

LIST #9. Words where the C is silent

<u>After a short vowel</u>	<u>After the S if followed by E or I</u>
back	scene
snack	scent
neck	science
deck	scimitar
slick	scissors
sick	crescent
sock	sciatica
rock	scintillating
stuck	scion
pluck	scepter
	scythe

Note: In *indict* (pronounced *in-dite*), the C is silent.

LIST #10. CE and CI with the SH sound

ocean	gracious
cetacean	luscious
crustacean	precious
	specious
	atrocious
	delicious
	conscious
	judicious
	malicious
	officious
	tenacious
	vivacious
	suspicious
	luscious
	crescendo

LIST #11. K before E or I

key	kid	kiosk
keel	kin	kindle
keen	kick	kidnap
keep	kill	kidney
kelp	kind	kipper
kept	kiln	kitten
ketch	king	kidding
kennel	kite	kilogram
kernel	kiss	kimono
kettle	kilo	kitchen
kelvins	kilt	kindness
ketchup	kink	kindergarten

3. The Silent E.

The most commonly used marker in English is the silent E. The spelling rule is simple, and students will quickly recognize it. The silent E indicates that the preceding vowel has changed from a short to a long vowel. Examples: *hop/hope, cap/cape, cut/cute.*

When adding a suffix, the problem is knowing when to drop the silent E:

Spelling Rule. Retain the silent E when a consonant suffix is used: *like/likeness, waste/wasteful.* See List #12.

Spelling Rule. Drop the silent E when a vowel suffix is used: *like/likable, waste/wasting.* See List #13.

Spelling Rule. Retain the silent E if the word ends in a soft C or soft G and will be followed by a hard vowel or a consonant: *nice/nicely, courage/courageous.* See List #14.

Drop the silent E in words that end in UE: *argue, argument, arguing.* See List #15.

Drop the silent E in words ending in DGE: *judgment, hedging.* See List #16.

Keep the silent E in words ending in OE: *hoeing, shoeing.* See List #17.

With short IE words, drop the silent E and change the I to Y: *tie/tying, die/dying.* See List #18.

Some of the consonant suffixes are *ly, ment, ness, less, ful,* and *ty.* Usually the silent E is retained, but there are exceptions.

LIST #12   **The silent E and suffixes retaining the E**

LY	MENT	NESS	LESS	FUL	TY
basely	basement	baseness	ageless	baleful	safety
absolutely	amusement	bareness	loveless	careful	ninety
abrasively	casement	oneness	priceless	eyeful	nicety
barely	movement	blueness	eyeless	rueful	surety
comely	pavement	cuteness	toeless	useful	naivety
cutely	agreement	hugeness	useless	woeful	subtlety
gamely	amazement	idleness	tieless	fateful	entirety
homely	atonement	lateness	clueless	gleeful	
hugely	elopement	likeness	fireless	hateful	
lamely	involvement	loneness	gateless	hopeful	

List 12 Continued

LY	MENT	NESS	LESS	FUL	TY
lately	placement	pureness	hopeless	tuneful	
likely	statement	rareness	homeless	wakeful	
lively	advisement	ripeness	lifeless	forceful	
lonely	bafflement	rudeness	nameless	graceful	
lovely	defilement	safeness	ruleless	grateful	
merely	effacement	sameness	shoeless	houseful	
mutely	engagement	soreness	timeless	peaceful	
namely	enticement	awareness	tireless	shameful	
nicely	management	crudeness	timeless	spadeful	
acutely	puzzlement	graveness	tireless	wasteful	
refinement	largeness	toneless	wireless	disgraceful	
bravely	settlement	staleness	brakeless	suspenseful	
closely	supplement	vagueness	graceless	spiteful	
crudely	achievement	politeness			
densely					
falsely					
gravely					
irately					

Also: able/ably, ample/amply, noble/nobly, bubble/bubbly, gentle/gently, agile/agily.

List #13. Drop the silent E

ING	ING	ABLE	IBLE
icing	dining	usable	forcible
dicing	mining	evadable	sensible
acing	tuning	notable	defensible
lacing	zoning	forgivable	collapsible
racing	droning	adorable	producible
dancing	aping	curable	convincible
cubing	doping	livable	reversible
lubing	hoping	erasable	erodible

List 13 Continued

ING	ING	ABLE	IBLE
bribing	piping	forgivable	sensible
robing	typing	closable	coercible
fading	wiping	hirable	submergible
hiding	boring	likable	reducible
knifing	caring	valuable	deducible
poling	curing	admirable	invincible
ruling	hiring	movable	tangible
baling	biting	arguable	evadible
coming	dating	solvable	corrodible
gaming	voting		
timing	tasting		
blaming	writing		

LIST #14. Retain the silent E

fiercely	gorgeous
nicely	courageous
hugely	advantageous
princely	outrageous
largely	rampageous
scarcely	umbrageous
savagely	
sagely	
strangely	

Note that although the silent E is very useful, there are times when it does not serve any useful purpose.

LIST #15. Words ending in UE

flue	flues		
cue	cued		
clue	clues		
due	dues		
hue	hues		
revue	revues		
rue	rueful	ruing	
sue	sued	suing	
blue	bluest	bluing	
glue	glued	gluing	
slue	slued	sluing	
true	truest	truing	
argue	argued	arguing	argument.
ensue	ensued	ensuing	
imbue	imbued	imbuing	
issue	issuer	issuing	
queue	queued	queuing	
pursue		pursued	pursuing

LIST #16. DGE words

badger	
fridge	
badge	badging
cadge	cadging
edge	edging
dredge	dredging
hedge	hedging
pledge	pledging
bridge	bridging
dodge	dodging
ridge	ridging
lodge	lodging

List 16 Continued

judge	judging	judgment
grudge	grudging	
smudge	smudging	
trudge	trudging	
nudge	nudging	
fledge	fledgling	
midget		
podgy		
budget		
drudgery		

LIST #17. OE words

doe	shoe
foe	canoe
hoe	
roe	
toe	
floe	
oboe	
sloe	
mistletoe	

LIST #18. Change I to Y

die/dying

lie/lying

tie/tying

vie/vying

4. U and V.

Apart from *you* and *flu*, no English word ends in U. But there are a number of imported or exotic words (loan words) that end in U. See List #19.

No commonly used English word ends with V.

LIST # 19.   Imported words ending in U

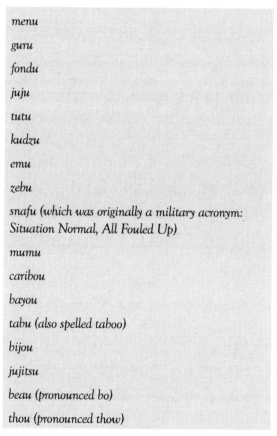

menu

guru

fondu

juju

tutu

kudzu

emu

zebu

snafu (which was originally a military acronym: Situation Normal, All Fouled Up)

mumu

caribou

bayou

tabu (also spelled taboo)

bijou

jujitsu

beau (pronounced bo)

thou (pronounced thow)

5. The Following R.

When a single vowel is followed by an R, the vowel becomes long. This new vowel sound is unique because many of the vowels sound the same and can confuse the student.

The UR sound: *fur, fir, her, worm, burn, bird, were, work.* See List #20.

The OR sound: *sword, born, worn.* See List #21.

The AH sound: *bar, arm.* This vowel sound sometimes also occurs with a following L, as in *palm* and *calm.* See List #22.

When the Y is followed by R, we can have three sounds: *pyrite, pyramid, myrtle.* See List #23.

But there is an anomaly: *bury* is pronounced *berry.*

LIST #20. The ER sound

UR	IR	ER
lurch	birch	perch
curt	dirt	pert
burst	birth	berth
fur	fir	her
blur	stir	term
hurt	shirt	herd
gurgle	squirm	external
turnip	third	permit
surgery	twirl	certain
murmur	flirting	concern

LIST #21. The OR sound

OR	OR	ORE
or	uniform	ore
for	transform	store
born	tortoise	wore
corn	torture	pore
cord	northern	ore
cork	record	more
pork	forgot	chore
lord	scorpion	before
morning	corpse	foreman
ordinary	storage	ignore

Notes: *Quarter* and *corps* (pronounced *core*) are the oddities in this group.

The OR sound can also be produced by vowel combinations discussed elsewhere.

LIST #22. The AR-AH sound

AR			AL
arc	arcade	target	palm
ark	barber	barley	calm
are	cardinal	garlic	alms
art	darling	partner	balm
arm	farmyard	remark	psalm
bar	hardware	gargle	qualm
car	partying	carnival	almond
arch	depart	farther	embalm

Some other words with that AH sound:

bra

ma

pa

spa

ah

hurrah

father

LIST #23. Three YR sounds

byre	myrtle	pyramid
gyre	myrrh	gypsies
gyro	satyr	Kyrie
lyre	martyr	lyric
pyre	zephyr	syrup
pyrite	Valkyrie	Egypt
papyrus		
styrene		
thyroid		

6. Soft and Hard G.

The G is similar to the C when it appears before soft and hard vowels. But there are exceptions. The difference between the C and the G is that sometimes the G is hard before the letters E and I, as in *get* and *give*.

Spelling Rule. The G is soft before Y and sounds like J: *gym*, *gypsy*. See List #24.

Spelling Rule. The G is usually soft before E and I, but at times it may be hard. Consider *giraffe* but *girl and gentle* but *get*. See List #25.

Spelling Rule. The G is hard before A, O, U, or a consonant: *gas, got, gun, green, glide, ghost*. See List #26.

When adding a suffix that begins with A, O, or U, or a consonant to a word that ends in GE, we must retain the silent E to keep the G soft: *manageable, encouragement*. See List #27.

When a word that ends in G must be followed by E or I, we often insert a U between the G and the soft vowel to keep the G hard: *guitar, guess*. See List #28.

LIST #24. Words using GY

clergy	edgy	gym
energy	elegy	gyp
eulogy	mangy	gyre
gypsum	rangy	orgy
gypsy	stagy	bulgy

LIST #25. Hard and soft GE and GI

HARD	SOFT	HARD	SOFT
get	gem	give	gin
geld	gent	gig	ginger
geek	germ	gift	gibe
gecko	genes	gild	giro (sometimes spelled gyro)
guest	genie	gill	giant

List 25 Continued

HARD	SOFT	HARD	SOFT
geisha	genre	gilt	gipsy
geyser	geode	gird	gist
gerbils	gelato	girl	giraffe
anger	gender	girth	gibbering
finger	genial	gizmo	gigantic
gear	genius	gibbon	
tiger	genome	girder	
begin	gentle	girdle	
corgi	gelatin	giggle	
	generic	gimmick	
	general	gigawatt	
	gesture	gizzard	

Notes: *Longevity* has a soft G: *lon-jev-i-ty*.

Gynecologist has one hard G (the first one) and one soft G (the second one).

LIST #26. Hard G

gun	gas
grin	gate
glut	got
leg	goat
pig	gum

LIST #27. Soft G retaining the silent E before A and M

forgeable	engagement
stageable	management
bridgeable	ravagement
changeable	impingement
chargeable	enlargement
manageable	arrangement
enlargeable	encouragement
salvageable	abridgement
marriageable	
knowledgeable	
interchangeable	

LIST #28. GU words with hard G sound

guide	argue	sanguine
guild	fugue	league
guilty	guess	guildhall
disguise	guest	colleague
guinea	rogue	guilelessly
guitar	vague	guerilla
anguish	vogue	
beguile	brogue	
languid	morgue	
penguin	plague	
roguish	tongue	

7. Double Consonants.

A very noticeable marker is the double consonant. The purpose of a double consonant is to warn us that the preceding vowel is short and the accent usually falls on the preceding syllable: *alley* but *ally*, *ballot* but *ballet*.

Spelling Rule. When adding a suffix, double the final consonant only if the word ends in a single consonant preceded by a short vowel and the suffix is a vowel suffix. The accent must be on the final syllable of the root word: *sitting, swimming, transmitting, runner.* See List #29.

The problem with double consonants is that over the years they have become unreliable markers. The rules that govern when and when not to double a consonant are complex and have numerous exceptions. Double consonants are thus the most serious impediment to good spelling. Explain to your students that a double consonant at the beginning of a word is often a prefix: **im**mobile, **un**necessary, **dis**satisfied, **in**nocent.

Many words also have double consonants that are not necessary: *commit, affect, appear, attract, immune, necessary.* See List #30.

There are about 150 commonly used words that have an unnecessary double consonant. There is also an equal number of words that should have double consonants.

LIST #29. Double-consonant words

cabbage	alley	collie	wallaby
rabbit	ally	dollar	swallow
ribbon	ballet	follow	wallet
hobby	ballot	hollow	wallow
abbey	challenge	jolly	pullover
daddy	gallery	lollipop	bullet
ladder	gallop	pollen	bulletin
traffic	rally	trolley	bullion
baggage	valley	bullock	pull
stagger	belly	clammy	bully
wedding	cellar	flammable	
effort	fellow	mammal	

List 29 Continued

beggar	intelligent	stammer
hidden	jelly	dilemma
difficult	trellis	glimmer
trigger	umbrella	simmer
shoddy	yellow	comment
coffee	artillery	commerce
office	billow	common
soggy	pillow	communist
rubber	brilliant	dummy
stubborn	gorilla	summer
pudding	pillar	mummy
sudden	pillow	summit
buffalo	vanilla	summon
ruffian	village	rummage
suffer	villain	suffocate
luggage	collar	rubbish
nugget	college	symmetry

LIST #30. Unnecessary double consonants

attract	committee	possess
dessert	assassin	occasion
arrange	accommodate	offend
appear	assessment	oppose
annoy	occurrence	paraffin
immune	address	parallel
aggressive	aggressive	personnel
affect	commence	recommend
accuse	commit	satellite
necessary	command	settee
immediate	connect	sufficient
arrest	collect	suggest
corruption	correct	supply

List 30 Continued

correct	collapse	support
allow	effect	suppose
addiction	assist	surrender
occur	embassy	surround
accordion	assemble	tattoo
accumulate	efficient	terrific
affect	arrive	torrential
announce	immense	irrigation
approach	interrupt	

8. K, CK, IC, AC.

Students are often puzzled to find words ending in C, K, or CK that all make the same sound. The spelling rules are logical and easy to remember.

Spelling Rule. The CK is used immediately after a short vowel: *sack, lock, thick*. See List #31

Usually, these are one-syllable words, but this group may also include multisyllable words when the syllable is closed or a suffix is added: *mimic/mimicking, slack/slacker*.

Spelling Rule. The K is used after long vowels and words that have a consonant after the vowel: *book, bank*. This includes words that need a silent E: *broke, take*. See List #30.

Spelling Rule. The C is used with multi-syllable words, especially words that end in IC and AC: *panic, insomniac*. Words ending in C sometimes add the K to keep the C hard when adding ing, ed, or L or AL because E and I are soft vowels: *panic/panicking, picnic/picnicker*. See List #31. BUT *public/publicity*.

Note that in the last few decades many exotic foreign words have been adopted into English. They often break the rules: *Sputnik, kayak, batik*. See List #32.

LIST #31. Some words containing CK, K, and C

sick	sink	epic		
sack	sank	antic		
sock	soak	attic		
suck	sunk	magic	magical	magicked
duck	punk	critic	critical	
back	pink	mimic	mimicking	mimicked
neck	perk	civic		
pick	park	panic	panicking	panicked
pack	bark	comic	comical	
brick	bank	frolic	frolicking	frolicked
chick	blink	cubic	cubical	
chuck	broke	picnic	picnicking	picnicked
kick	ink	cynic	cynical	

List 31 Continued

lock	look	ethic	ethical
cocktail	hawk	mosaic	
backpack	broke	logic	logical
wicked	book	garlic	garlicky
chicken	chink	lyric	lyrical
clock	cloak	public	
gecko	monk		medic	medical
bucket	shrink	lunatic	
cuckoo	hawk	music	musical
hockey	think	optic	optical
packet	rank		psychic
reckon	coke	topic	topical
attack	tank	toxic	
barracks	rank	arctic	
dock	duke	atomic	
jockeys	joke	basic	
speckled	speak	fabric	
unlucky	like	apologetic	
kickback	bake	agnostic	
pockmark	poke		insomniac
reckless	dunk		fanatic

LIST #32. Exotic words ending in K

schnook	aardvark
trek	kerplunk
geek	sputnik
kulak	punk
kapok	refusnik
anorak	beatnik
batik	chinook
mukluk	gemsbok
kayak	neatnik

9. CH and TCH.

Your students will grasp these rules very quickly.

Spelling Rule. TCH is used after a short vowel. TCH is used mainly in single-syllable words, but when it is used in multi-syllable words, it will be part of a short vowel syllable: *itch, featherstitching.* See Lists #33 and 34.

Spelling Rule. CH is used after a long vowel or a consonant: *each. voucher. inch.* See list #34.

But there are a number of anomalies. See List #35

List #33. TCH with a short vowel

etch	hutch
itch	ketch
batch	latch
bitch	letch
botch	match
butch	notch
catch	patch
ditch	pitch
Dutch	watch
fetch	witch
fitch	blotch
hatch	crutch
hitch	hopscotch

List #34. CH with a long vowel or a consonant

LONG VOWEL	VOWEL WITH CONSONANT
ouch	inch
coach	bench
couch	arch
leach	church

List 34 Continued

LONG VOWEL	VOWEL WITH CONSONANT
mooch	torch
peach	ranch
pouch	punch
poach	porch
beach	birch
vouch	bunch
touch	filch
teach	finch
roach	pinch
reach	gulch
mooch	larch
leech	lunch
	lurch
	lynch
	march
	mulch
	munch
	parch
	perch

List #35. Anomalies using CH

sandwich	bachelor
ostrich	duchess
detach	rich
attach	which
such	much

10. J, GE, DGE.

This is another common marker that confuses students because these letter combinations all sound more or less alike.

Spelling Rule. Except for a few exotic imports, J is never used at the end of an English word: *hadj* or *hajj*, *raj*. Note that *hadj* and *hajj* are Arabic words. *Raj* comes from *Hindi*.

Spelling Rule. Use GE if the word has the long vowel sound or if there is a consonant following the vowel: *huge*, *range*. See List #36.

Spelling Rule. Use DGE if the word is a short vowel word and there is no consonant following the vowel: *judge*, *badge*. See List #36.

These words will usually be single-syllable words, but there are also a few multisyllable words: *knowledge. curmudgeon.* See List #36

When adding a suffix that begins with a hard vowel (A, O, U) or a consonant, we would normally retain the final silent E. But when the DGE is used, we drop the E because the digraph DG has the J sound: *judgment.* See List #37.

LIST #36. DGE and GE

SHORT VOWEL	LONG VOWEL OR CONSONANT + G	
edge	age	siege
badge	cage	singe
budge	gage	stage
cadge	huge	surge
dodge	page	tinge
fudge	rage	usage
hedge	sage	verge
judge	urge	allege
ledge	wage	avenge
lodge	barge	change
nudge	beige	charge
ridge	bilge	dotage

List 36 Continued

SHORT VOWEL	LONG VOWEL OR CONSONANT + G	
sedge	hinge	deluge
wedge	bulge	emerge
bridge	damage	engage
dredge	forge	flange
drudge	gauge	fringe
fridge	gouge	garage
grudge	large	sponge
pledge	mange	lounge
smudge	merge	manage
trudge	purge	refuge
hodgepodge		

List #37. Words with DG that drop the E

judge	judging	judgment
abridge	abridging	abridgment
acknowledge	acknowledging	acknowledgment
edge	edging	
budge	budging	
cadge	cadging	
lodge	lodging	lodgment
nudge	nudging	

Note: Nearly all short DGE words drop the E when adding ING.

Part Two: Working with Consonants

𝒴our students will understand the sounds of the consonants quickly and should have little difficulty using them once they learn the various ways they can be used.

11. Changing Y to I.

The following rules are used when forming plurals and when adding suffixes.

Spelling Rule. If there is a vowel before the Y, just add the S or the suffix: *boy/boys*, *play/playful*. See List #38.

Spelling Rule. If there is a consonant before the Y, change the Y to I before adding the plural ES or the suffix: *baby/babies*, *sky/skies*, *happy/happily*. See List #38.

If the suffix begins with I, retain the Y to avoid a double I. *baby/babyish*, *pity/pitying*.

When adding OUS, most words change the Y to I: *victory/victorious*, *luxury/luxurious*. But there is a group that changes the Y to E for no discernable reason: *courtesy/courteous*, *beauty/beauteous*. See List #39.

A few words ending in AY change the Y to I after the vowel when forming the past tense: *lay/laid*, *say/said*. See List #40.

LIST #38. Some words that change the Y to I

VOWEL BEFORE THE Y		CONSONANT BEFORE THE Y	
boy	boys	baby	babies
toy	toys	daddy	daddies
coy	coyly	hanky	hankies
joy	joyful	happy	happily
play	player	sloppy	sloppiest
tray	trays	cry	cried
slay	slaying	merry	merrily
clay	clayey	sky	skies

List 38 Continued

VOWEL BEFORE THE Y		CONSONANT BEFORE THE Y	
key	keyed	bury	buried
buy	buyer	cozy	coziest

LIST #39. EOUS

pity	piteous
plenty	plenteous
beauty	beauteous
bounty	bounteous
miscellany	miscellaneous
courtesy	courteous

LIST #40. AY/AID

lay	laid
pay	paid
say	said (but pronounced sed)

12. QU plus a vowel.

This is an easy one for your students. Since there are no exceptions to the following rule, any word we run across where the Q stands alone is a foreign word, probably translated from Arabic or Chinese, which have different alphabets and sounds.

Spelling Rule. In English spelling, the Q may not stand alone. Excluding names, the Q must always be followed by a U and a vowel. There are no exceptions. See List #41.

The QU has the KW or CW sound, but no commonly used English word starts with either of these combinations. Your dictionary may show the word *cwm*, but this is a Welsh word pronounced *koom* and meaning a small valley or a large hollow on the side of a hill. It was brought into English as the suffix *combe*, which is used in place names like Buncombe.

LIST #41. QU

aqua	aquarium	acquire
quad	quay	quid
quip	quit	quiz
equal	equipment	quack
quake	queen	queue
quick	quite	quiet
quaint	quartz	quench
quilt	quota	sequel
sequin	square	squeak
squirt	unique	acquire
banquet	baroque	bouquet
equator	equinox	liquidate
quarrel	quarter	

Note: In a few English words, the QU is pronounced K: *mosquito, picturesque, antique, physique.*

13. AL, TIAL, CIAL.

Many nouns can be made into adjectives by the addition of the suffix AL: *logic/logical, coast/coastal*. But sometimes it is necessary to preserve or create a soft S sound before the AL. So we insert an I before the AL. *part/partial, race/racial*.

Spelling Rule. Most words in this group end in TIAL. This includes all words that come from a root that ends in T: *torrent/torrential, president/presidential*. See List #42.

Spelling Rule. Words that come from a root that ends in a soft C use the CIAL ending: *office/official, social, crucial*. See List #43.

Spelling Rule. Most words that come from a root that ends in ENCE or ANCE use TIAL: *essence/essential, confidence/confidential*. See List #44.

Note: There are some anomalies: *palace/palatial, space/spatial, axe/axial, equinox/equinoctial*.

LIST #42. TIAL

initial	partial
spatial	martial
impartial	celestial
existential	palatial
inertial	evidential
potential	essential
substantial	residential
presidential	influential
differential	confidential
circumstantial	prudential
torrential	exponential

LIST #43. CIAL

facial	racial
social	crucial
glacial	fiducial
special	official
judicial	artificial
financial	commercial
beneficial	prejudicial
provincial	superficial
sacrificial	

LIST #44. TIAL in words ending in ENCE or ANCE

sequence	sequential
substance	substantial
confidence	confidential
circumstance	circumstantial
residence	residential
essence	essential
preference	preferential
credence	credential
evidence	evidential
prudence	prudential
deference	deferential
existence	existential
influence	influential
reverence	reverential
penitence	penitential
difference	differential
pestilence	pestilential

14. EFY. IFY.

This is a very easy one. The verb suffix FY means "to make or to become." *Solidify*, for example, means "to make solid."

Spelling Rule. The ending IFY is used in almost all the words in this group. Examples: *identify*, *amplify*. See List #45.

Note that the ending EFY is used with only three words: *putrefy, stupefy, tumefy*. These three exceptions can be traced back to Latin roots. Fortunately, they are rarely used words.

LIST #45. IFY

deify	*unify*
citify	*codify*
modify	*notify*
pacify	*purify*
ratify	*uglify*
beautify	*beatify*
certify	*dignify*
falsify	*glorify*
horrify	*justify*
magnify	*mummify*
mystify	*signify*
specify	*zombify*

Note: These words lead to other words:

putrefy	*putrefaction*
stupefy	*stupefyingly*
tumefy	*tumefaction*

15. SEED, CEDE, CEED, SEDE.

There are few words that use these endings, but they are confusing because they come to us from different Latin roots.

Spelling Rule. The spelling SEED is only used for seed, including its compounds and derivatives: *seedling, linseed*. See List #46.

Spelling Rule. Almost all the other words use CEDE. Example: *concede*. See List #46.

Two other possible endings are CEED and SEDE. Only four words use CEED: *exceed*. Only one word uses SEDE: *supersede*. See List #46.

When the long EE sound is changed to a short E sound, it will be spelled with only one E: *excess, success, procession*.

Note that *emceed* is a new word. It is the past tense of *emcee*, which is formed from the abbreviation MC, or Master of Ceremonies. This word first appeared during the 1930s.

LIST #46. SEED, CEED, SEDE, CEDE

SEED	CEDE	CEED	SEDE
seed	cede	succeed	supersede
seeding	recede	exceed	
reseed	secede	proceed	
seedling	accede	emceed	
linseed	antecede		
aniseed	intercede		
	precede		
	concede		

16. ER, OR, AR, RE, OUR.

These five endings pose no great problem because Noah Webster eliminated both the British RE (*theatre/theater*) and OUR (*labour/labor*) from American spelling, which solved the whole problem.

Spelling Rule. The ER ending is mainly used for occupations or for persons who carry out an action: *runner, baker.* See List #47.

Note that some exceptions end in OR: *jailor, chancellor.* See List #47.

There are also a few words that still end in RE so that they will conform to the soft and hard C and G rules: *acre, ogre.* See List #48.

Spelling Rule. The OR ending is used with root words that end in T or S: *actor, divisor.* See List #49.

Some words end in OUR, but they have different sounds: *detour, your, devour, our.*

Spelling Rule. Many of the words ending in AR are adjectives: *circular, regular.* See List #50.

Note that comparative adjectives usually end in ER: *sad/sadder, quick/quicker.*

There are many nouns that also end in AR: *dollar, seminar.* See List #51.

LIST #47. ER and OR

ER	ER	OR	OR
butcher	writer	governor	donor
eater	teacher	juror	author
lawyer	jumper	emperor	jailor
baker	banker	sponsor	warrior
driver	maker	assessor	conqueror
drinker	porter	purveyor	tailor
absolver	abstainer	survivor	aggressor
auctioneer	biographer	councilor	mortgagor
bartender	blender	professor	ambassador
carpenter	carrier	supervisor	chancellor
climber	comforter		

ER	ER	OR	OR
dweller	embalmer		
fertilizer	fielder		
grumbler	hacker		
importer	informer		
moocher	modernizer		
adviser	conjurer		

List 47 Continued

LIST #48. RE

acre

ogre

lucre

mediocre

wiseacre

massacre

LIST #49. TOR and SOR

TOR	TOR	SOR	SOR
actor	reactor	assessor	sensor
tutor	realtor	compressor	processor
bettor	senator	sponsor	aggressor
cantor	visitor	confessor	depressor
doctor	adjustor	oppressor	possessor
editor	agitator	precursor	professor
mentor	ancestor	successor	supervisor
orator	creditor	predecessor	repossessor
suitor	defector	divisor	microprocessor
victor	dictator		
adaptor	director		
auditor	educator		
aviator	imitator		
creator	impostor		

47

List 49 Continued

TOR	TOR	SOR	SOR
curator	inflator		
donator	inventor		
ejector	mediator		
erector	operator		
janitor	sculptor		
monitor	vibrator		

LIST #50. AR in adjectives

near	clear
solar	linear
circular	vulgar
angular	bipolar
insular	jocular
regular	secular
similar	tubular
cellular	binocular
columnar	globular
peculiar	molecular

Note: These words sound alike but have different meanings:

sailer - sailor
censer – censor
quitter – quittor
lumber – lumbar
hanger – hangar

For more words that sound alike, see the section on homophones and List #151.

LIST #51. AR in nouns

jaguar	vinegar	altar
grammar	hangar	calendar
cougar	collar	caterpillar
scholar	dollar	grammar
vicar	pillar	caviar
nectar	mortar	cellar
cedar	guitar	

17. RY, ARY, ERY, ORY, URY, IRY, RRY.

These seven endings can be quite confusing. Explain to your students that they are all variations of the RY suffix. Examples: *hairy, solitary, watery, armory, treasury, wiry, cherry, cheery.*

Spelling Rule. Most of the words in this group use the root word followed by RY: *silver/silvery, burglar/burglary.* See List #52.

Note: The silent E is sometimes dropped: *injure/injury, wire/wiry.*

The vowel before the RY is sometimes dropped: *anger/angry, hunger/hungry.* See List #53.

Many of the words that end in ARY are adjectives: *solitary, temporary.* See List #54.

Spelling Rule. Many of the words that end in ERY are nouns that describe a workplace: *surgery, tannery.* See List #55.

Root words ending in ER add a Y to become adjectives: *water/watery, blubber/blubbery.* See List #56.

Most words that end in ORY follow a T or an S: *victory, advisory.* See List #57.

There are only a few words that end in URY: *luxury, perjury.* See List #58.

There are only a few words that end in IRY: *inquiry, airy.* See List #59.

Not many words use the double R, which occurs after a short vowel: *carry, sorry.* See List #60.

LIST #52. RY

airy	buttery	furry
hoary	teary	armory
blurry	eatery	fakery
finery	floury	flowery
poetry	savory	smeary
sugary	vapory	watery
winery	bigotry	archery
brewery	bribery	cannery
silvery	burglary	injury
hairy	belfry	bravery
starry		

LIST #53. Dropped vowels

anger/angry	hunger/hungry
psalter/psaltery	enter/entry
scare/scary	winter/wintry
chanter/chantry	launder/laundry
register/registry	ancestor/ancestry
minister/ministry	

LIST #54. ARY in adjectives

wary	scary	weary	
bleary	dreary	sugary	dietary
primary	unitary	contrary	culinary
honorary	literary	ordinary	salutary
sanitary	solitary	tertiary	vinegary
ancillary	auxiliary	budgetary	customary
exemplary	fiduciary	imaginary	legendary
mandatary	mercenary	momentary	necessary
planetary	residuary	secondary	sedentary
temporary	tributary	visionary	voluntary

LIST #55. Workplace words ending in ERY

surgery	tannery	bakery	eatery
winery	brewery	cannery	grocery
hosiery	joinery	piggery	pottery
slavery	tannery	colliery	creamery
delivery	hatchery	refinery	saddlery
chandlery	costumery	millinery	perfumery

LIST #56. ERY in adjectives

watery	blubbery	every	fiery
cheery	fakery	finery	misery
papery	jittery	bravery	dithery
flowery	peppery	powdery	quavery
quivery	rubbery	shivery	showery
silvery	spidery	blistery	blustery
feathery	flickery	fluttery	glittery
leathery	savagery	shimmery	slippery
slithery	thundery	twittery	whispery

LIST #57. ORY with T or S

WITH T	WITH T	WITH S
victory	accusatory	cursory
factory	statutory	illusory
history	signatory	elusory
oratory	repertory	sensory
rectory	refectory	advisory
auditory	purgatory	delusory
lavatory	predatory	accessory
adulatory	migratory	compulsory
crematory	mandatory	precursory
directory		promissory
dormitory		supervisory

LIST #58. URY

fury	augury
perjury	mercury
luxury	jury
usury	floury
injury	treasury
century	bury
penury	

Note that "bury" is pronounced *berry*.

Note also that "penury" is pronounced *pen-yury*.

LIST #59. IRY

airy

inquiry

hairy

dairy

fairy

miry

wiry

LIST #60. RRY

starry	carry
scurry	hurry
slurry	sherry
berry	furry
merry	blurry
curry	sorry
cherry	worry
quarry	marry
ferry	

18. LY, LLY, ALLY.

The LY suffix is used to change an adjective into an adverb: *quick/quickly, slow/slowly*.

Spelling Rule. In the majority of cases, we simply add LY to the root word: *firm/firmly, astonishing/astonishingly*. See List #61.

If the root ends in L, we retain the L when adding LY: *final/finally, graceful/gracefully, cool/coolly*. See List# 62.

Spelling Rule. If the root word ends in AL, the suffix must be ALLY: *final/finally, emotional/emotionally*. See List #63.

Words ending in IC must use ALLY to retain the hard C: *music/musically, dramatic/dramatically*. See List #64.

Note that in most cases the silent E is retained: *close/closely, wide/widely*. See List #65.

Words ending in LE simply change the E to a Y: *terrible/terribly, horrible/horribly*. See List #66.

Spelling Rule. Change the Y to I before adding the suffix: *happy/happily, pretty/prettily*. See List #67.

But there is a small group of single syllable words that do not change the Y to I: *shy/shyly, sly/slyly*. See List #68.

LIST #61. Words that end in LY

firmly

astonishingly

shortly

lately

quickly

slowly

loudly

silently

LIST #62. LL retaining the second L

lawfully	gracefully
evilly	foully
awfully	civilly
woefully	irefully
artfully	sinfully
joyfully	usefully
coolly	woefully
fitfully	bashfully
cruelly	basically
manfully	dutifully
tinselly	fretfully

LIST #63. Words that end in ALLY

finally	really
royally	casually
loyally	totally
orally	locally
annually	dismally
brutally	genially
equally	legally
frugally	fatally
actually	globally
morally	usually
dually	regally
ritually	specially

LIST #64. C before the suffix

focally	locally
rascally	basically
magically	medically
stoically	topically
clinically	critically
ironically	mythically
vocally	fiscally
ethically	publicly
comically	cynically
logically	musically
optically	radically
typically	chemically
cosmically	cyclically
heroically	myopically
physically	vertically
statistically	

LIST #65. Words that end in ELY

barely	basely	finely	gamely
lamely	lately	lonely	lovely
nicely	palely	rudely	safely
comely	cutely	wisely	acutely
homely	hugely	likely	lively
insanely	merely	namely	ornately
purely	rarely	politely	immensely
sorely	widely		

LIST #66. Words that end in BLY

terribly	horribly	doubly	feebly
rumbly	wobbly	curably	lovably
legibly	pliably	adorably	bearably
ably	nobly	bubbly	pebbly
humbly	nimbly	affably	amiably
movably	notably	dribbly	credibly
visibly	trembly	volubly	deniably
flexibly			

LIST #67. Words that end in ILY

happily	prettily	drily	gaily
icily	bodily	cagily	cozily
angrily	crazily	gaudily	giddily
juicily	luckily	daily	hazily
busily	cozily	easily	gamily
dizzily	fancily	huskily	jollily
merrily	nastily	noisily	

LIST #68. Words that keep the Y before LY

coyly	dryly
spryly	shyly
slyly	wryly
gayly	

19. ABLE, IBLE.

The suffix IBLE is a variant of ABLE. These suffixes are used to create adjectives: *depend/dependable*, *sense/sensible*.

Spelling Rule. Add ABLE to the whole root word: *eat/eatable*, *wash/washable*. See List #69.

Spelling Rule. Words that end in S or T will usually use IBLE: *reverse/reversible*, *convert/convertible*. Note that words ending in a soft C or soft G will usually use IBLE: *forcible*, *tangible*. See List #70.

Spelling Rule. Words ending in a silent E usually drop the silent E, especially when it follows a soft C or soft G: *reduce/reducible*, *submerge/submergible*. See List #70.

Spelling Rule. If the root ends in a soft C or soft G, it must retain the silent E if the suffix is ABLE: *notice/noticeable*, *knowledge/knowledgeable*. See List #71.

Spelling Rule. If the root word ends with Y, we must change the Y to I and use ABLE: *rely/reliable*, *envy/enviable*. See List #72.

Spelling Rule. If the root word ends in a hard C or hard G, it must use ABLE: *implacable*, *navigable*. See List #73.

If the root word can accept the suffix ATE or ATION, we must use ABLE: *tolerate/toleration/ tolerable*, *tax/taxation/taxable*. See List # 74.

If the root word can accept the suffix ION but not ATION, we must use IBLE: *collect/collection/ collectible*. See List #74.

LIST #69. ABLE

doable	actable	drinkable	eatable
mixable	ownable	seeable	sewable
arguable	bankable	farmable	feedable
addable	buyable	dryable	fixable
flyable	payable	rowable	bearable
sowable	skiable	taxable	savable
chewable	cashable	foldable	

LIST #70. IBLE with S, T, G, or C

corruptible	convertible	legible	invincible
fusible	ignitible	eligible	fencible
visible	comestible	fungible	forcible
feasible	compatible	dirigible	producible
possible	digestible	frangible	reducible
sensible	deductible	tangible	crucible
reversible	ingestible	illegible	inducible
invisible	resistible	incorrigible	irascible
accessible	revertible	negligible	
immersible	combustible	submergible	
impossible	exhaustible	intelligible	
implausible	suggestible		
comprehensible			

LIST #71. ABLE words that retain the E

forgeable	stageable	chargeable	manageable
unbudgeable	exchangeable	camouflageable	discourageable
adduceable	balanceable	displaceable	serviceable
embraceable	enforceable	influenceable	irreplaceable
pierceable	placeable	renounceable	replaceable
serviceable	sliceable	bridgeable	changeable
enlargeable	salvageable	marriageable	rechargeable
interchangeable	knowledgeable	danceable	defaceable
divorceable	effaceable	enticeable	forceable
noticeable	peaceable	pronounceable	reinforceable
retraceable	unpronounceable	traceable	

LIST #72. Words that change the Y to I and ABLE

deniable	dutiable	reliable	variable
notifiable	notifiable	verifiable	certifiable
rectifiable	satisfiable	enviable	pitiable
unifiable	modifiable	pacifiable	remediable
falsifiable	qualifiable	specifiable	vitrifiable

LIST #73. Hard C or hard G plus ABLE

amicable	navigable
revocable	huggable
applicable	fatigable
extricable	litigable
irredicable	delegable
evocable	propagable
medicable	singable
eradicable	hangable
communicable	indefatigable
educable	
allocable	
despicable	
replicable	
practicable	
impeccable	
implacable	
explicable	
incommunicable	

LIST #74. TION or SION with ABLE or IBLE

citation–citable	admission-admissible
notation–notable	fusion-fusible
adoration–adorable	evasion-evadible
education–educable	deduction-deductible
fixation–fixable	reduction-reducible
salvation–salvable	vision-visible
adoration–adorable	tension-tensible
mutation-mutable	division-divisible
taxation–taxable	infusion-infusible
damnation–damnable	accession-accessible
gradation–gradable	erosion-erodible
isolation– isolable	coercion-coercible
ignition-ignitable	eruption-eruptible
operation-operable	omission-omissible
expiation/expiable	

20. TION, SION, SSION, TIAN, CIAN, CION, SHION, XION, SIAN, CEAN.

These suffixes—all pronounced *shun*— are usually used to turn a verb into a noun. The syllable can be spelled in ten different ways, but, interestingly, there is no commonly used word, apart from the word *shun* itself, that uses SHUN as an ending.

Spelling Rule. The majority of words in this group use the TION ending: *attention, fraction.* See List #75.

Spelling Rule. The suffix SION is a variation of TION and is usually used after roots ending in D. and S with a silent E: *pretend/pretension, averse/aversion.* See List #76.

Words ending in double S will be spelled SSION: *confess/confession, express/expression.* See List #76.

Words ending in MIT will also use the double S: *admit/admission, permit/permission.* See List #77.

Words ending in CEDE and CEED will also use the double S: *secede/secession, proceed/procession*

Spelling Rule. The CIAN ending is almost always used to indicate a trade, skill, or profession: *magician, technician, beautician.*

The TIAN ending is similar to CIAN, but usually indicates a place of origin or a belief: *Martian, Dalmatian, Christian.* See List #78.

Fewer than half a dozen words use XION: *crucifixion, transfixion.*

Three other rare spellings are *ocean, cetacean, cushion, fashion, suspicion, coercion.* See List #79.

LIST #75. TION

action	auction	potion	lotion	option
diction	duration	reflection	notation	ruination
function	gyration	ovation	gyration	location
junction	jubilation	ovulation	hibernation	motion
mention	nation	ignition	bastion	emotion
portion	quotation	inaction	edition	fiction
selection	solution	quotation	taxation	
caption	fraction	traction	vocation	

LIST #76. D, S, SS

D	S	S	S	SS
elide	elision	erase		confession
elude	elusion	tense	tension	accession
erode	erosion	effuse	effusion	regression
evade	evasion	averse	aversion	obsession
explode	explosion	submerse	submersion	recession
persuade	persuasion	precise	precision	remission
abrade	abrasion	suffuse	suffusion	concussion
allude	allusion	converse	conversion	digression
decide	decision	convulse	convulsion	discussion
delude	delusion	disperse	dispersion	impression
deride	derision	televise	television	expression
divide	division	transfuse	transfusion	oppression
invade	invasion	circumcise	circumcision	possession
ascend	ascension			profession
corrode	corrosion			regression
pretend	pretension			

LIST #77. MISS

submit – submission

emit – emission

transmit – transmission

omit – omission

manumit – manumission

admit – admission

remit – remission

permit – permission

commit – commission

LIST #78. CIAN, TIAN

magician	musician	Venetian
logician	optician	Egyptian
physician	tactician	titian
politician	technician	tertian
cosmetician	electrician	Martian
obstetrician	pediatrician	gentian
theoretician	arithmetician	fustian
pediatrician	dietician	Christian
mortician	beautician	Dalmatian
academician	logistician	Lilliputian
statistician	diagnostician	

LIST #79. Other spellings

complexion	ocean
effluxion	cetacean
fluxion	crustacean
crucifixion	panacean
transfixion	cushion
fashion	scion
coercion	suspicion

21. LE, EL, AL, IL, OL, UL, YL.

When explaining these ending to your students, point out the difference between ANGEL and ANGLE. (They should not be eating *angle-hair* pasta!)

Spelling Rule. If the main part of the word ends in a soft C or a soft G, it cannot be followed by LE or AL. It must use EL: *cancel, angel.* See List #80.

Spelling Rule. If the main part of the word ends in a hard C or a hard G, it cannot be spelled EL. It must use either LE or AL: *miracle, bugle, frugal.* See Lists #81, 82, and 83.

Spelling Rule. The majority of words ending in AL are adjectives: *colossal, vertical.* Note that words ending in a silent E will loose the E before AL: *tide/tidal, brute/brutal.* See Lists #83, 84, and 85.

Spelling Rule. Most words ending in CLE or CKLE are nouns: *vehicle, buckle.* See Lists #86 and 87.

Note that the following consonants are usually followed by LE: B, D, F, G, P, Z. Examples are *table, paddle, shuffle, giggle, apple, puzzle.*

The following consonants are **never** followed by LE: M, N, R, V, W: *normal, enamel, signal, tunnel, choral, barrel, arrival, shovel, renewal, towel.*

The YL is found mainly on scientific words: *ethyl, pterodactyl.* See List #88.

Very few words end in UL (if we exclude diphthongs and words ending in FUL): *consul.* See List #88

If we exclude diphthongs, fewer than two dozen words end in IL: *anvil, pupil.* See List #88.

Many of the words that end in OL are chemical terms: *ethanol, petrol.* See List #88.

LIST # 80. Soft C and soft G ending with EL

cancel	*angel*
parcel	*cudgel*
chancel	
ensorcel	

List #81. Hard C ending with LE

uncle	canticle	muscle	cycle
oracle	tabernacle	carbuncle	article
cuticle	tentacle	chronicle	debacle
recycle	obstacle	particle	treacle
clavicle	barnacle	binnacle	follicle
pinnacle	vehicle	corpuscle	popsicle
spectacle	monocle	pentacle	receptacle
circle	manacle	miracle	icicle

List #82. Hard G ending with LE

angle	bangle	bungle	burgle
tangle	finagle	gurgle	haggle
juggle	jungle	ogle	quadrangle
beagle	boggle	dangle	draggle
gaggle	gargle	mingle	jingle
mangle	mingle	rectangle	shingle
bugle	eagle	goggle	jangle
octangle	wriggle		

List # 83. Hard C ending with AL

decal	focal	rascal	bifocal
ethical	logical	musical	optical
anatomical	biblical	ironical	mythical
tactical	tropical	legal	regal
conjugal	madrigal	local	vocal
comical	cubical	lyrical	magical
radical	topical	chemical	clinical
physical	poetical	vertical	classical

List #84. Hard G ending with AL

frugal	fungal	prodigal	centrifugal
cynical	fiscal	medical	typical
cyclical	surgical	graphical	paralegal
regal	madrigal	legal	conjugal

LIST #85. AL words that drop the silent E

tidal	brutal	ducal	fatal
usual	anodal	urinal	primal
accusal	disposal	algal	final
tonal	tubal	bridal	clonal
spinal	spiral	exposal	figural
basal	modal	clonal	global
tribal	perusal		

LIST #86. Words ending with CLE

cycle	uncle	muscle	oracle
cuticle	pentacle	chicle	circle
article	bicycle	tricycle	chronical
icicle	coracle	chronicle	receptacle

List 87. Words ending with CKLE

shackle	buckle	knuckle	truckle
crackle	chuckle	pickle	nickel
speckle	trickle	spackle	prickle
tickle	suckle	heckle	fickle
tackle	freckle	sickle	cockle

LIST #88. Words ending with YL, UL, IL, OL

YL	UL	IL	OL
alkyl	karakul	anvil	petrol
ethyl	annul	civil	argol
hexyl	mogul	devil	vitriol
vinyl	bulbul	evil	thiazol
butyl	consul	fossil	retinol
isopropyl		lentil	menthol
pterodactyl		nostril	naphthol
		pencil	alcohol
		peril	ethanol
		basil	cholesterol
		gerbil	
		April	
		vigil	
		tranquil	
		utensil	
		stencil	
		pupil	
		Brazil	

22. IZE, ISE, YZE.

Explain to your students that while these endings are suffixes, not all words with these endings have suffixes. The difference is where the speaker puts the accent when saying the words. Good pronunciation is a great help here.

Spelling Rule If the ending is an unaccented final syllable, that syllable will probably be a suffix and will be spelled IZE: *criticize, specialize*. See List #89.

Note that YZE is mainly restricted to scientific words: *hydrolyze analyze*. See List #90.

Spelling Rule If the final syllable is accented, that word is probably a whole word and will be spelled ISE: *revise, surprise*. See List #91.

But there are many exceptions to the rule. Words that end in ISE mainly come from three groups:

a. Words that end in WISE: *unwise, otherwise*.

b. Words that end in VISE or CISE: *advise, excise*.

c. Words that end in RISE or MISE: *comprise, surmise*.

LIST #89. IZE

iodize	ionize	agonize	anodize
atomize	ebonize	itemize	odorize
realize	activize	botanize	canonize
demonize	deputize	equalize	eulogize
humanize	idealize	maximize	memorize
moralize	motorize	sanitize	satirize
elegize	idolize	oxidize	stylize
alkalize	amortize	civilize	colonize
digitize	energize	vaporize	finalize
immunize	legalize	minimize	mobilize
organize	polarize	criticize	

LIST #90. YZE

analyze	catalyze
electrolyze	paralyze
breathalyze	dialyze
hydrolyze	

LIST # 91. ISE

unwise	advise	endwise	devise
edgewise	revise	likewise	televise
sidewise	supervise	clockwise	improvise
otherwise	surprise	excise	arise
incise	demise	exercise	surmise
exorcise	apprise	reprise	crosswise
sunrise	comprise	lengthwise	streetwise

Note: Anomalies include *assize, capsize, prize, seize, baize, concise, promise, precise, premise.*

23. ICAL, ACLE, ICLE.

The difference between ACLE and ICLE depends on the origin of the word, usually a Latin root word. There is no rule that divides words with these endings into two groups, so your students will just have to memorize them.

Spelling Rule. Words ending in ICAL are almost always adjectives: *musical, clinical.* See List #92.

Spelling Rule. Words ending in ACLE and ICLE are almost always nouns: *obstacle, cubicle.* See List #93.

No commonly used English word ends in CUL, and only a tiny handful end in COL, CIL, or CEL: *protocol, pencil, cancel.* See List #94.

LIST # 92. ICAL adjectives

musical	clinical	comical	logical
conical	cubical	cynical	ethical
lyrical	magical	medical	musical
optical	radical	stoical	topical
typical	chemical	biblical	clerical
critical	cyclical	inimical	mystical
mythical	nautical	theoretical	surgical
tactical	tropical	vertical	

LIST #93. ACLE and ICLE nouns

oracle	chicle	coracle	icicle
barnacle	article	binnacle	cubicle
debacle	cuticle	manacle	radicle
miracle	vehicle	obstacle	canticle
pentacle	clavicle	pinnacle	follicle
receptacle	particle	spectacle	popsicle
tabernacle	chronicle	tentacle	testicle
treacle	ventricle		

LIST #94. COL, CIL, CEL

COL	CIL	CEL
col	pencil	parcel
glycol	stencil	cancel
caracol	council	carcel
protocol	codicil	marcel
		excel
		chancel
		tercel

24. ANT, ENT, ANCE, ENCE, ENSE.

Hundreds of words end in ENT or ANT. Generally speaking, the majority of the words that end in ENT tend to be adjectives, whereas a large number of words that end in ANT tend to be nouns. But this is by no means a general rule.

Spelling Rule. After a hard C or a hard G, the suffix will be ANT: *applicant. fumigant.* See List #95.

Spelling Rule. After a soft C or a soft G, the suffix will be ENT: *magnificent, urgent.* See List #96.

Generally, the suffix ANT indicates a person or thing that does something and will probably be a noun: *contestant, occupant.* But there are numerous exceptions. These two are adjectives: *significant, resistant.* See List #97.

Generally, the suffix ENT indicates a quality or characteristic. It will probably be an adjective: *excellent, efficient.* But there are numerous exceptions: *shipment, tenement.* See List #98.

Note that not every word that ends in ENT or ANT has a suffix: *cement, current, plant, currant.*

Many words end in ENSE. They tend to be a mixture of nouns and adjectives: *license, intense.* See List #99.

Many words end in ENCE. They tend to be nouns: *absence, difference.* See List #99.

LIST #95. CANT, GANT

	CANT	GANT
cant	significant	elegant
scant	communicant	arrogant
decant	supplicant	fumigant
recant	mendicant	litigant
vacant	lubricant	termagant
intoxicant	desiccant	congregant
applicant		extravagant

One anomaly is *sergeant.*

LIST #96. CENT, GENT

recent	adolescent	agent
accent	complacent	urgent
ascent	quiescent	regent
descent	subjacent	pungent
decent	fluorescent	tangent
docent	magnificent	indigent
decent	obsolescent	diligent
percent	translucent	insurgent
crescent	luminescent	divergent
indecent	acquiescent	detergent
innocent	munificent	intelligent

LIST #97. ANT words, mostly nouns

occupant	claimant	significant	resistant
contestant	aspirant	chant	implant
errant	debutant	extant	oxidant
mutant	emigrant	infant	odorant
pedant	immigrant	pliant	pageant
tenant	habitant	vacant	peasant
truant	merchant	adamant	servant
coolant	applicant	buoyant	vagrant
defiant	assailant	currant	warrant
migrant	assistant	elegant	tolerant

LIST #98. ENT words, mostly adjectives

different	present	innocent	prominent
excellent	efficient	eloquent	insolent
recent	lenient	prudent	intelligent
eminent	resident	evident	confident
silent	consistent	sufficient	continent
patient	imminent	competent	tenement
transient	permanent	persistent	incident
shipment	accident	accent	accomplishment
achievement	adjacent	agreement	advertisement

LIST #99. ENSE, ENCE words, mostly nouns

sense	fence
dense	hence
tense	whence
offense	silence
intense	absence
license	science
defense	reference
incense	essence
expense	existence
immense	patience
nonsense	opulence
dispense	audience
pretense	commence
condense	prudence
suspense	sentence
recompense	insolence
commonsense	impudence

Part Three: Working with Vowels

*B*ecause of the wide variety of spellings for similar sounds, vowels are the main problem for anyone learning how to spell English words. This is especially true when the same vowels arranged in the same order can produce different sounds, as in *you, though, bough,* and *cough.* There should be no great problem with the consonants, but the English vowel sounds and diphthongs can be a major stumbling block for any student because all the vowels can have more than one sound.

The logical way to tackle this problem is to concentrate on the sounds of the vowels and diphthongs. The students should study groups of words that sound alike and are spelled alike. (word families) This is the most efficient way to acquire long-term memory.

Try this sentence on your students. It is a twenty word sentence with eleven A sounds and six different spellings.

> *They say that the vain and lazy Dane was slain when it rained for eight days straight during his reign.*

Any student who can correctly spell every word in this sentence clearly understands how varied English spelling is.

THE VARIOUS SOUNDS OF A.

The letter A has four basic sounds (the short sound and the A+E, AI, AR sounds), but these sounds can be spelled in well over a dozen different ways, as explained below.

25. The short A and A + silent E.

The short A is the most common A in English. It is usually the first vowel taught to beginning students with sentences such as *The cat sat on the mat*. See List #100.

Combining the short A with the silent E, produces a long vowel sound and therefore creates a new word. For example, *pan* (short A) becomes *pane* (long A). See List #101.

LIST #100. Short A

and	angle	after	path	thank	sank
ant	candle	rather	daft	rattle	package
bat	handle	advance	craft	ghastly	mask
bag	tangle	draft	avalanche	than	wax
cat	dangle	graft	banana	raffle	contrast
can	scramble	raft	bastard	raspberry	slam
crab	strangle	shaft	drama	chat	rabbit
camp	apple	branch	example	baffle	mast
damp	grapple	chant	flabbergast	brass	dazzle
drank	cattle	piano	panorama	catch	van
fat	axle	plant	rascal	dabble	stamp
flag	mangle	slant	strata	glass	paddle
flat	ramble	bath	paddle	match	past
glad	trample	ask	saddle	backtrack	trap
grand	black	straddle	bask	class	straggle
hand	sack	blast	ham	cash	tax
jack	cask	jam	lack	cashbox	saddle
cast	land	pack	castleman	grass	task
smack	clasp	pan	smack	flash	vast
fast	plan	snack	flask	flashing	
rat	track	gasp	mass	smash	
rang	tracker	grasp	smashed	pass	
sad	tracking	last	disaster	tackle	

78

The short A is not a big problem and has only a few oddities:

1. *Giraffe* has the short A but an unnecessary E at the end.

2. *Avalanche* also has an unnecessary E at the end.

3. *Lather* has the short A, but *father* has the AH sound.

4. *Armada* has two A's that have the AH sound. The third A is short.

5. *Staff* and *graph* both have the short A sound.

6. *Cast* and *caste* (both pronounced *kast*) both have the short A sound.

7. *Salmon* has the short A sound and the L is silent.

8. *Salami* has two A sounds.

LIST #101. A + silent E

fad/fade	wag/wage	cradle	promenade	gave	ladle
cap/cape	tap/tape	stable	vase	grade	table
dam/dame	stag/stage	fable	ape	hate	gable
at/ate	slat/slate	able	bale	lake	cable
fat/fate	sham/shame	fate	baby	lane	wave
gal/gale	scrap/scrape	fame	bake	made	wake
gap/gape	rat/rate	fake	blade	male	trade
glad/glade	rag/rage	face	blame	name	tame
hat/hate	plan/plane	date	brake	page	take
lath/lathe	pan/pane	crave	brave	place	stale
mad/made	pal/pale	crater	cage	quake	spade
man/mane	nap/nape	crate	cake	race	snake
mat/mate		cave	came	safe	same

Oddity: *Have.* The silent E is not needed.

26. AI, AY, EI.

This long A sound can be spelled in five ways. Here are the three most common.

a. The majority of words containing the AY sound use the A plus the silent E: *made, rate.*

b. The second most common group uses the AI: *maid, rain.*

c. The third common group uses AY: *may, ray.*

Spelling Rule. The AI spelling is used in the middle of a word. The AI must be followed by at least one consonant, as in *paid* and *raid.* There are very few anomalies. See List #102.

Spelling Rule. The AY spelling is used at the end of a word: *delay, replay.* See List #103.

There are very few words that start with AI or AY. *aid, aide, ailing, aim, aye,* and the Persian word *ayatollah.*

When adding suffixes, the Y is **not** usually changed to I, except for three words: *say/said* (BUT remember that "said" is pronounced *sed*), *pay/paid, lay/laid.* See List #103.

Another, less common, way to create the AY sound is by using EI: *eight, vein.* See List #104.

There are also a few words that use EY, or the ET for the AY sound at the end of a word: *fey, bouquet.* See List #105.

LIST #102. AI

paid	raid	aim	air	said
bait	jail	braid	fair	plait
brain	gain	grain	lair	kaiser
afraid	faint	chains	pair	mosaic
dainty	daisies	failed	cairn	archaic
maiden	obtain	praise	chair	liaison
retail	vainly	assail	dairy	samurai
bailiff	braised	claimed	fairy	villain
contain	derail	exclaim	flair	
failure	gaining	mailbox	stair	
nailing	ordain	painful	affair	
plainly	praised	prepaid	impair	
ptomaine	refrain	rainbow	affair	

80

LIST #103. AY

delay	replay	away	clay
gray	sway	slay	today
allay	array	decay	delay
essay	relay	spray	today
subway	waylay	midday	dismay
betray	affray	hooray	sashay
astray	defray	mislay	parlay
giveaway	disarray	soothsay	takeaway
hideaway	mainstay	stairway	horseplay
quay (BUT pronounced kee)			

LIST #104. EI

rein	vein	veil	skein
freight	reign	deign	feign
neigh	eight	weigh	weight
neighbor	sheik	beige	sleigh
feign			

LIST #105. EY, ET at the end of a word

fey	ballet
obey	beret
prey	bidet
they	buffet
survey	cabaret
purvey	bouquet
convey	cabriolet
whey	cachet
trey	chalet
	crochet
	croquet
	duvet
	parquet

27. AU, AW, OU, ALL.

The AWE sound can be spelled in a number of ways.

Spelling Rule. The AU spelling will be found in the middle or at the beginning of a word: *cause, audience*. See List #106.

The AU spelling only appears at the end of a few words that are mainly of French origin: *plateau, bureau, trousseau*.

Spelling Rule. The AW spelling will be found at the end of a word or syllable: *straw, outlaw*. See List #107.

The AW sometimes appears before a final N or L: *lawn, drawl*. See List #107.

Very few words begin with the digraph AW: *awkward, awful*.

There are also two small groups of words that produce the AW sound using the spellings AUGH (*daughter*) and OUGH (*fought*). See List #108.

There is a small group of words that use the double L after the A: *fall, call*. See List #109.

LIST # 106. AU

auditor	sauce	haul
audible	maul	daub
augment	taut	fraud
auspice	cause	pause
author	fault	vault
audio	daunt	gaunt
auger	haunt	jaunt
auto	launch	paunch
auburn	staunch	faucet
august	faun	gaudy
aurora	caulk	jaunt
autocracy	mauve	sauna
autograph	bauble	caucus
authority		

82

audience

aura

auction

LIST #107. AW, often followed by L or N.

jaw	trawl	lawn
paw	shawl	dawn
law	drawl	fawn
haw	awl	pawn
raw	crawl	sawn
saw	yawl	spawn
yaw	prawn	bylaw
straw	drawn	jigsaw
squaw	brawn	outlaw
flaw	yawn	
thaw	awe	
gnaw	awful	
claw	awning	
draw	awkward	
macaw	awesome	

LIST #108. AUGH, OUGH

aught	ought
caught	fought
daughter	bought
distraught	thought
fraught	brought
haughty	sought
taught	wrought
naught	besought
naughty	
slaughter	

List 106 Continued

LIST #109. A before LL

all	stall
fall	befall
call	squall
tall	install
ball	appall
gall	recall
hall	thrall
wall	nightfall
small	overall

28. AR.

The AR can be used anywhere in a word and is usually spelled with the letters AR: *artist, barn, guitar*. See List #110.

The AR spelling usually gives us the AH sound: *arm, charm*. BUT the AH sound is sometimes spelled with the letter L, which is silent: *palm, calm*. See List #110.

In most of the southeastern part of England, it is fashionable to pronounce many words with the AH we hear in *car* and *star*, (*pahssport, bahth, Irahn*). This way of speaking was originated by the upper class and the landed gentry during the 19th century as a way of distinguishing themselves from the lower classes. It was quickly copied by the middle class and soon became the accepted way to speak in certain parts of England and on the BBC. Throughout the rest of England, in North America, and in much of the English-speaking world, the spelling rule is followed: when the A is in a closed syllable, it is short, as in *cat* and *hat*. When the vowel is followed by a double consonant, it has to be a short vowel. The only time the A has the AH sound is when it is followed by R, or sometimes the L. There are very few exceptions.

LIST #110. AR and AL

artist	barn	guitar	calm
arm	charm	ajar	balm
army	barge	char	palm
argue	cards	spar	embalm
armor	alarm	scar	napalm
arcade	darning	star	psalm
ardent	farmer	tsar	qualm
arsonist	apartment	bazaar	
artist	dartboard	cigar	
archer	barking	radar	
armada	barley	caviar	
armadillo	carpet		

29. AIR, ARE, EAR, ERE, ERR, EIR.

The AIR sound can be spelled in six ways.

The largest group of words use AIR to get the AIR sound: *airplane, affair.* See List #111.

A similar group of words use ARE: *care, stare.* See List #112.

A few words use EAR: *bear, pear.* See List #113.

Some words use ERE: *there, where.* See List #113.

And two words use EIR: *heir, their.*

LIST #111. AIR

airplane	dairy	affair	airport
fair	hair	pair	unfair
cairn	chair	dairy	impaired
airier	fairest	mohair	chairman
repair	unfair	airfare	despair
prairie	corsair	despair	solitaire
upstairs	airborne	éclair	

LIST #112. ARE

care	aware
stare	beware
glare	cookware
fare	compare
bare	daycare
dare	declare
hare	ensnare
mare	fanfare
pare	flare

rare	hardware
share	nightmare
wares	prepare
spare	square

List 112 Continued

LIST #113. EAR, ERE

bear	there
pear	derriere
tear	where
wear	somewhere
bearer	elsewhere
forbear	anywhere
bearable	nowhere
swimwear	ere
unbearable	

30. AL, ALL.

When the A is followed by a single or double L, there are two possible sounds and four spellings.

1. The regular short A sound with one L: *alphabetical, California.*

2. The regular short A sound with two L's: *rally, ballad.*

3. The AUL sound with one L: *also, walk.*

4. The AUL sound with two L's: *ball,. fall.* See List #114.

LIST #114. ALL (double L)

allow	ballot	call
ally	mallet	gall
allay	gallop	stall
alley	pallet	appall
alloy	tallow	squall
dally	shallow	all
shall	valley	wall
rally	allege	hall
tally	sallow	tall
ballet		pall
galley		fall
ballad		ball
hallow		small
allied		befall
pallid		recall
		mall

THE VARIOUS SOUNDS OF E.

E is the most often used letter in the English language and can produce a wide variety of sounds and spellings.

The **short E** should be no problem for your students. Examples: *get, set. ten, men.*

31. IE, EI.

Words using IE and EI should not be a problem if the student is taught to listen to *the sounds* of the words. You should teach your students this old rhyme:

> I before E.
>
> Except after C.
>
> Or when sounding like AY in *neighbor and weigh.*
>
> Or when sounding like EYE in *seismic and height.*

Spelling Rule. Use I before E if the word has the long E sound. But it must be a true diphthong: *niece, believe.* See List #115.

There are a few anomalies like *friend* and *sieve.*

Spelling Rule. Except after C: *ceiling, deceive.* But this does **not** include plurals or comparatives.

There are a few anomalies: *conscience, efficient.*

Spelling Rule. Or when sounding like AY. There are a number of words that are spelled with EI but sound like AY: *eight, freight.* See List #116.

Spelling Rule. Or when sounding like EYE. Many of these words have been borrowed from the German: *Fahrenheit, poltergeist.* See List #117.

There are a number of anomalies: *sovereign, counterfeit.*

LIST #115. The EE sound spelled IE or EI.

IE	IE	IE	EI
field	pier	grief	ceiling
shield	cashier	fief	receipt
wield	siege	pierce	receive
believe	thief	achieve	deceit
chief	yield	belief	deceive
mischief	tier	priest	conceit
hygiene	bier	chief	perceive
piece	diesel	shriek	conceive
niece	reprieve		seize
relief	relieved		
brief	.		

LIST #116. The AY sound spelled EI

eight	veil
freight	surveillance
deign	heinous
weigh	eighty
beige	eighteen
neighbor	inveigh
vein	inveigle
feign	lei
weight	seine
neigh	sheik
reign	chow mein
reins	feint
reindeer	obeisance
skein	dreidel
sleigh	geisha

LIST #117. EI pronounced like the long I

height	heist
Rottweiler	seismic
apartheid	feisty
eidetic	gneiss
stein	poltergeist
Einsteinium	kaleidoscope
Fahrenheit	sleight
edelweiss	Pleistocene
zeitgeist	Geiger counter
sleight	gesundheit

32. EA, EE.

It is fascinating to see just how many ways there are to produce the long E sound in English spelling. A teacher could spend an entire class period just counting the ways.

Spelling Rule. The EA and the EE are mostly used in the middle of a word: *beat, beet.* See List #118.

Not many words start with EA: *eat, each.* Nor do many words end with EA: *tea, sea.* See List #119.

Very few words begin with EE: *eel, eerie.*

Many words end with EE: *knee, pedigree.* See List #120.

In a number of words, the long E sound is produced by a single E: *zero, region.*

Some words (most from the French) are spelled EE but pronounced with the long A: *toupee.* See List #121.

Sometimes the long E is produced by a single E supported by the silent E at the end of the word: *extreme, complete.*

LIST #118. EE, EA

EE	EA
beet	beat
agreement	appeal
beehive	beady
cheeky	cheating
discreet	displease
feeble	features
geese	greasy
heel	healing
jeering	jeans
kneeling	kneading
leeway	leader
meetinghouse	mealtime

EE	EA
needlework	neatness
overseer	upstream
peeling	peaceful
queen	queasy
refreeze	reseal
screech	scream
tweeting	tweaking
unfeeling	wheat
veneer	yeast
wheedling	
zookeeper	

List 118 Continued

LIST #119. Words that start or end with EA

eat	pea	earn	area
each	lea	early	idea
ears	sea	earth	urea
ease	tea	earnest	apnea
east	flea	earl	azalea
easy	plea		cornea
eaves	guinea		nausea
eager			panacea
eagle			diarrhea
easel			miscellanea
Easter			bougainvillea

LIST #120. Words that end with EE

bee	fee	see	tee	flee	free
glee	knee	thee	tree	agree	payee
three	apogee	coffee	decree	degree	goatee
pedigree	settee	amputee	evacuee	foresee	Frisbee
jubilee	nominee	oversee	referee	chimpanzee	

List #121. Words from the French ending in EE

melee

puree

soiree

toupee

33. Y, EY, I, EE, IE as word endings.

All these have the same basic EE sound

Spelling Rule. The EE ending is usually produced by Y: the final syllable of *baby, easy.*

Almost any word can be made into an adjective by adding the Y: *blood/bloody, careful/carefully.*

Some words use EY. They will usually have the EE sound (*money*) but also sometimes the AY sound (*prey*).See List #122.

Some words end in I. These are often Italian words like *salami* and *ravioli*. But also: *tsunami, bikini.* See List #123.

Most of the EE words describe a person or position: *referee, trainee.* And some words end in IE: *goalie, zombie.* See List #124.

LIST #122. Two basic sounds of EY

key	trolley	they
abbey	paisley	fey
alley	odyssey	obey
boney	journey	prey
cagey	chimney	convey
dopey	valley	bey
honey	turkey	purvey
money	pulley	disobey
nosey	mousey	survey
barley	monkey	
donkey	medley	
galley	lackey	
hockey	kidney	
jersey		
jockey		

LIST #123. Two sounds of I

ski	psi
yeti	rabbi
mini	radii
taxi	alkali
semi	alumni
deli	cacti
khaki	fungi
okapi	
bikini	
salami	
safari	
macaroni	
pastrami	
spaghetti	
confetti	
ravioli	
chili	

LIST #124. EE, IE referring to a person

emcee	trustee	goalie
payee	absentee	zombie
adoptee	employee	newbie
advisee	enrollee	bookie
amputee	licensee	cabbie
awardee	appointee	
devotee	consignee	
draftee	franchisee	
escapee	retiree	
evacuee	refugee	
evictee	referee	
grantee	invitee	
honoree	trainee	

THE VARIOUS SOUNDS OF I

The letter I has a number of sounds and there are many ways to spell those sounds. Students should have no trouble with the short I, as a large number of words use it: *in, it, tin, bin.* The short I is usually in a closed syllable: *dig, spring.*

34. LONG I.

There is a small group of words that have the long I sound. In most of these words the I is followed by N or L.: *wild, mind.* See List #125.

LIST #125.   The long I sound

child	*wild*
mild	*mind*
blind	*behind*
kind	*hind*
rind	*grind*
find	*bind*
Rhine	rhinoceros

35. IR.

When the I is followed by an R, it has the UR sound: *fir, stir.* But, when the R is preceded by a diphthong, words ending in IR will not always have the UR sound. See List #126.

LIST #126. Different spellings of IR sounds

fir	*air*	*heir*	*weir*
sir	*fair*	*their*	*nadir*
stir	*hair*	*tapir*	
thirty	*lair*	*elixir*	
whir	*flair*	*Kashmir*	
bestir	*pair*	*souvenir*	

36. I + silent E.

When the I is followed by a silent E, it will have the long I sound: *fire, stripe*. But there are a few words in which the silent E is used but is not really needed and does not produce the long I sound: *imagine, primitive*. See List #127.

LIST #127. Various sounds of I + silent E

imagine	primitive	noise
engine	give	poise
famine	olive	raise
marine	active	chaise
cocaine	motive	cruise
examine	native	praise
genuine	captive	valise
moraine	festive	malaise
opaline	massive	mortise
		promise
		bruise
		porpoise
		practice

37. IGH. IGN.

A small group of words use the GH or the GN to get the long I sound: *sigh, sign*. See List #128.

LIST # 128. IGH, IGN

sigh	sign
nigh	align
high	assign
thigh	benign
	design
	cosign
	realign

38. The Y sound.

There are a number of commonly used words where the Y has the long I sound: *hyena, nylon*. See List #129.

LIST #129. Y as the long I sound

ply	tying
pry	cycle
try	lying
sty	type
cry	byline
dye	flying
bye	gynecology
fry	hypothesis
sly	lifestyle
why	hydraulic
psychiatry	hyper
dehydration	nylon
formaldehyde	hyena
dynamics	
hydro	
pyromaniac	

THE VARIOUS SOUNDS OF O

The O is one of the most frequently used letters in English spelling. It can be found in over a dozen combinations.

Many words use the short O: *hotpot, obnoxious.*

39. THE LONG O.

At the end of a word, the O will have the long sound: *zero. buffalo.* See List #130.

LIST # 130. The long O sound

zero	audio	buffalo	cargo
domino	cameo	ago	ditto
ego	tango	tyro	limbo
typo	albino	halo	grotto
veto	tuxedo	echo	potato
zero	tomato	also	fiasco
lasso	indigo	hippo	stucco
banjo	poncho	polio	weirdo
motto	kimono	piano	pseudo
video	ghetto	radio	stereo

The double OO has four sounds. See List #131.

a. *zoo, too*
b. *book, look*
c. *door, floor*
d. *blood. flood*

LIST #131. Four OO sounds

zoo	book	floor	blood
boom	cook	boor	flood
cool	foot	poor	
fool	good		
doom	brook		
boot	hood		
food	hook		
goof	nook		
tool	soot		
loom	took		
moon	wood		
noon	wool		
roof	crook		
room	hoof		
root	look		
tooth			
troop			

The long O can be spelled in a variety of ways. Be prepared to take a lot of time and insist on careful pronunciation.

40. O + E, OA, OW, OE.

The most common spelling uses the silent **E**: *hope, rope*. But almost as many words use the **OA** combination or the **OW** to get the same or a similar sound: *boat. soap, row, throw*.

Spelling Rule. The OA is usually used in the middle of a word: *goat, road*. See List #132.

Spelling Rule. The OW is usually used at the end of a word. It does not change with suffixes or compounds: *yellowish, blowing*. See List #133.

A small group of words use the **OE** to get a similar sound: *toe,. foe*. See List #134.

LIST #132. OA

goat	road	boat	coat
coal	coax	foal	foam
goal	goat	load	loaf
oak	oath	roam	soak
soap	toad	boast	cloak
coast	croak	float	foam
gloat	groan	moan	loan
poach	roast	soak	soap
toad	toast		

LIST #133. OW

low	throw	blow	widow
yellow	window	mow	pillow
row	borrow	sow	fellow
tow	follow	crow	hollow
flow	meadow	glow	shadow
grow	willow	know	rainbow
show	shallow	slow	sparrow
stow	swallow	arrow	bungalow
below	hedgerow	elbow	overthrow

LIST #134. OE

toe	foe
doe	hoe
roe	aloe
sloe	pekoe
mistletoe	oboe
floe	

41. The OR/ORE sound

Spelling Rule. The most common spelling is the plain OR: *order, actor.*

Spelling Rule. The ORE spelling is also common, but it is used only at the ends of words: *before, store.* See List # 135.

LIST #135.   ORE

ore	bore
store	core
before	fore
more	gore
lore	pore
sore	tore
wore	adore
chore	score
shore	snore
spore	store
swore	ashore
before	encore
ignore	anymore
deplore	explore
eyesore	implore
onshore	restore
folklore	pinafore
sycamore	seashore
carnivore	fourscore
semaphore	sophomore

42. OU.

This diphthong can be very confusing. It has many different sounds. Among them are *you, out, source*. See List #125.

Spelling Rule. The OU spelling is usually used in the middle of a word: *hour. astound.*

OU is almost never used at the end of a word with few exceptions: *you, caribou.* See List #136.

A few words begin with OU: *out, ounce.* See List #137.

LIST #136. OU sounds

you	caribou		contour	source
coup	acoustics	flour	blouse	four
loupe	carousel	foul	account	pour
bayou	gourmet	hour	mouth	court
could		loud	county	gourd
uncouth		noun	doubt	mourn
ghoul		about		bought
group		impound		fought
cougar		bound		brought
douche		couch		sought
dour		foul		courtly
detour		cloud		mourning
famous		found		ought
nougat		mount		
bivouac		mouse		
youth		noun		

List #137. OU at the beginning of a word

ouch

out

ounce

our

ours

ourselves

ousted

outbid

outhouse

Spelling Rule. The OW is usually used at the end of a word: *how, now, cow*. Very few words begin with OW: *owe, own*. See List #138.

LIST #138. OW at the beginning of a word

owl	owlish		
owe	owed	owner	owing

43. OY, OI

Spelling Rule. The OY is used at the end of a word: *boy, enjoy.*

Spelling Rule. When the OI is used in the middle of a word, it must be followed by at least one consonant: *point, boil.* See List #139.

Note that *OID* is a suffix meaning "like": *asteroid, spheroid.*

Very few words begin with OI: *oil, ointment.*

When adding suffixes to OY words, the Y is *not* usually changed to an I: *employer, toying.*

LIST #139. OI

koi	oil
boil	coil
coin	foil
join	loin
roil	soil
toil	void
avoid	broil
coin	droid
foist	groin
hoist	moist
point	spoil
poise	anoint
voice	boiler
foist	poison
quoits	toilet
appoint	anoint
choice	rejoice
noise	devoid

LIST #140. Four words from the French, one two-syllable OI word

coif (a French word, the OI is pronounced WAH)

soiree (a French word, the OI is pronounced WAH)

chamois (a French word sometimes pronounced *shammy*)

memoir (a French word, the OI is pronounced WAH)

heroic (here the OI is two syllables)

choir (rhymes with wire)

44. OUGH

Many words have this archaic ending that can produce five different sounds, which is all very confusing to students. Examples: *thought, through, although, bough,* and *cough.* See List #141.

LIST #141. Five ways to pronounce OUGH

bough	dough	rough	thought	through
sough	though	tough	ought	
slough	borough	enough	fought	
doughty	although	cough	sought	
drought	furlough	trough	brought	
	thorough		bought	
			besought	
			wrought	

THE VARIOUS SOUNDS OF U.

Both the long and the short U sound can be spelled in a number of ways. Students often confuse the long U with the long OO sound.

45. THE SHORT U.

The short u can have two sounds: *but, cut,* and also *bull, pull.* See List #142.

LIST #142. Short U (note the double l)

but	bull
buck	pull
bun	cull
bud	full
bug	gull
buff	hull
budge	mull
bum	null
bun	dull
bus	lull
but	scull
buzz	skull

46. U+ silent E.

A number of words use the silent E with the U to get a slightly different sound: *pure, cure.* See List #143.

Usually the U + silent E produces a long U sound: *flute, include.* See List #144.

LIST #143. URE, UE, EW

pure	fracture	cue	dew
cure	failure	hue	few
sure	feature	due	new
lure	fixture	sue	knew
azure	gesture	argue	pew
allure	lecture	ensue	stew
assure	leisure	issue	drew
demure	measure	pursue	curfew
endure	mixture	queue	mildew
insure	pasture	rescue	nephew
ensure	picture	revue	aircrew
figure	posture	subdue	preview
future	procure	tissue	purview
injure	rupture	value	interview
manure	seizure	barbecue	review
mature	texture	avenue	screw
nature	torture	fescue	
secure	venture	statue	
suture	vulture	virtue	
capture	aperture	revenue	
denture	exposure	devalue	
		blue	
		true	

LIST #144. U+ silent E

cube	puce
nude	huge
duke	mule
plume	dune
cure	lube
truce	ruder
refuge	fluke
rule	spume
tune	pure
muse	mute
flute	fuse
include	

47. UI.

A small group of words use the UI to get a long U sound: *fruit, juice.* See List #145.

LIST #145. UI

fruit

suit

cruise

juice

bruise

sluice

recruit

48. EU, EW, EAU.

Sometimes these combinations make the long U sound: *feudal, jewel, beauty*. See List #146. Words that end in EAU usually come from the French.

LIST #146. EU, EW, EAU

EU		EW	EAU	French words
lieu	feud	jewel	beauty	beau
euro	deuce	shrew	beautiful	gateau
pseudo	queue	screw		bureau
rheumatism	eulogy	crew		tableau
eunuch	eureka	new		chateau
milieu	neuron	few		plateau
neuter	pneumonia	dew		
sleuth	voyeur	drew		
amateur	liqueur	grew		
masseur	neutral	pew		

Another EAU word is *bureaucracy*.

49. OUS, EOUS, IOUS, UOUS.

Roughly half of the most commonly used English words that end in US have one of these endings. They all have the US sound. See List #147.

Spelling Rule. If the root ends in a consonant, use the simple OUS: *marvel/marvelous*.

Spelling Rule. If the root word ends in a silent E, drop the E: *nerve/nervous, fame/famous*.

Spelling Rule. If the root word ends in a soft G followed by a silent E, the E is retained to protect the G, but it is still silent: *courage/courageous, outrage/outrageous*.

A small group of words use the EOUS spelling for no logical reason: *bounteous, beauteous*.

Spelling Rule. If the root ends in a soft C followed by a silent E, the E is changed to I and has the SH sound: *grace/gracious, space/spacious*.

A number of words with Latin roots use IOUS with the SH sound: *conscious, ambitious, obnoxious*.

Spelling Rule. If the root ends in Y, change the Y to I. The new word will have the long E sound: *vary/various, envy/envious*.

Spelling Rule. If the root ends in U, the U is retained and is always pronounced clearly: *virtue/virtuous, impetuous*.

If the root ends in F, it will change to a V: *grief/grievous, mischief/mischievous,*. Note that *mischievous* has only *three syllables*, not four: *MIS/che/vus*

LIST #147. Varieties of OUS

OUS	IOUS	EOUS	UOUS	VOUS
jealous	anxious	gaseous	arduous	
nervous	bilious	hideous	fatuous	grievous
odorous	copious	igneous	tenuous	mischievous
ominous	curious	piteous	sinuous	
onerous	devious	gorgeous	innocuous	
ruinous	dubious	nauseous	vacuous	
zealous	envious	beauteous	sensuous	
covetous	furious	bounteous	tortuous	
cumbrous	noxious	courteous	unctuous	

List 147 Continued

OUS	IOUS	EOUS	UOUS	VOUS
cumulus	obvious	erroneous	virtuous	
decorous	tedious	righteous	ambiguous	
desirous	various	miscellaneous	congruous	
enormous	vicious	spontaneous	impetuous	
fabulous	factious	instantaneous	tempestuous	
generous	glorious	extraneous	strenuous	
grievous	ambitious	courageous	sumptuous	
humorous	luscious	outrageous	continuous	
infamous	pervious	aqueous	tumultuous	
libelous	precious	curvaceous	conspicuous	
luminous	gracious	plenteous	ingenuous	
marvelous	spacious	simultaneous	contemptuous	
dangerous	conscious		mellifluous	
nervous	ambitious		promiscuous	
famous	obnoxious		contiguous	
mischievous	salacious		deciduous	
	previous		voluptuous	
	delicious		assiduous	
	rebellious			
	serious			
	superstitious			
	notorious			
	hilarious			
	ferocious			
	studious			
	victorious			

ANNOYING SPELLINGS

Over the centuries, the English language has acquired an extraordinary number of words from a wide variety of other languages. It is safe to say that our dictionaries contain words borrowed from almost every language under the sun—from French, German, Arabic, and ancient Greek to the multiple languages of China, of India, and Australian aborigines.

It is therefore not surprising that English contains a large number of words with awkward and sometimes illogical spellings. Since English is the only major language that has no official Academy or Committee (like the Académie Française) that controls the language, these irregular spellings and oddities simply continue to exist, much to the annoyance and confusion of students both domestic and foreign who are trying to learn correct English.

There are too many irregularities for me to list them all. They range from unnecessarily doubled consonants to strange vowel sounds. Below are lists of words that begin with an unnecessary consonant that makes it is impossible for students to look these words up in the dictionary if they don't know what the first letter is. See List #148.

For good measure, I have also listed words that contain the unlovely and archaic *ough*, *augh*, and *igh* spellings that should have been abandoned centuries ago. See Lists #149 and 150.

50. Silent First Letters

List #148. Silent first letters

<u>G</u>	<u>H</u>	<u>K</u>	<u>M</u>	<u>P</u>	<u>W</u>
gnu	hour	knack	mnemonic	pneumatic	wrap
gnaw	honor	knit		psychic	wrest
gnash	heir	knob		psychedelic	wreath
gnome	herb	knot		pterodactyl	wrath
gnocchi	honest	knowledge		pterosaur	wrack
gnat		knee		pneumonia	wriggle
gnarl		knickers		psychology	wren
gnawn		knead		psychopath	whole
gneiss		knoll		ptarmigan	wrestle
gnosis		knight		pseudo	wring
gnostic		knell			wrangle

List 148 Continued

G	H	K	M	P	W
		knock			wretch
		knuckle			writhe
		knew			wrung
		knout			write
		knapsack			wrench
		know			wreak
		kneel			wretched
					wreck
					wrinkle
					wrong
					wrist
					writ
					wrought
					wry

51. The GH Words

List #149. GH words (with varied pronunciations)

OUGH		AUGH	IGH	
bough	although	aught	high	nigh
sough	ought	caught	sigh	bight
plough	bought	naught	night	plight
slough	fought	taught	light	sprightly
drought	thought	fraught	right	neigh
cough	brought	haughty	tight	deign
rough	sought	daughter	flight	feign
tough	borough	slaughter	fight	reign
enough	furlough	distraught	knight	weigh
trough	thorough	laugh	sight	inveigh
dough	through	draught	slight	sleigh
doughy	hiccough		delight	neighbor
though				

Note that some of these words are obsolete or spelled more simply in the U.S.: *plough/plow,* *hiccough/hiccup, draught/draft.*

List #150. EIGHT and AIGHT

freight	straight
eight	
height	
sleight	

121

52. Confusing Homophones

Homophones are words that sound alike but have different meanings: *affect/effect, past/passed*. They're mostly pairs, but there are also a few triplets: *to/too/two*. English has about 400 homophone pairs whose definitions need to be clearly explained to your students: *its* is a possessive adjective, whereas *it's* is a contraction of "it is." See List #151.

List #151. Common homophones and their parts of speech

affect / effect	*affect: verb / effect: noun*
past / passed	*past: adverb / passed: verb*
than / then	*than: conjunction or preposition / then: adverb*
which / witch	*which: pronoun / witch: noun*
here / hear	*here: adverb / hear: verb*
are / our	*are: verb / our: possessive adjective*
buy / by	*buy: verb / by: preposition*
weather / whether	*weather: noun / whether: conjunction*
you're / your	*you're: contraction of "you are" / your: possessive pronoun*
bear / bare	*bear: noun or verb / bare: adjective or verb*
one / won	*one: number or pronoun / won: verb*
brake / break	*brake: noun or verb / break: noun or verb*
complement / compliment	*complement: verb / compliment: verb*
aloud / allowed	*aloud: adverb / allowed: past tense verb*
its / it's	*its: possessive adjective / it's contraction of "it is"*
right / write	*right: adverb / write: verb*
piece / peace	*piece: noun / peace; noun*
capital / capitol	*capital: adjective / capitol: noun*
principal / principle	*principal: adjective and noun / principle: noun*

new / knew	new: adjective / knew: past tense verb
hear / here	hear: verb / here: adverb
deer / dear	deer: noun / dear: adjective or noun
cereal / serial	cereal: noun / serial: adjective or noun
course / coarse	course: noun / coarse: adjective
die / dye	die: verb / dye: verb
fair / fare	fair: adjective / fare: noun
flour / flower	flour: noun / flower: noun
heal / heel	heal: verb / heel: noun
hole / whole	hole: noun / whole: adjective
hour / our	hour: noun / our: possessive adjective
idle / idol	idle: adjective / idol: noun
patience / patients	patience: noun / patients: plural noun
canvas / canvass	canvas: noun / canvass: verb
mantle / mantel	mantle: noun / mantel: noun
seen / scene	seen: past participle / scene: noun
sweet / suite	sweet: adjective / suite: noun
feint / faint	feint/ noun or verb / faint: noun or verb
size / sighs	size: noun / sighs : verb
sun / son	sun: noun / son: noun
see / sea	see: verb / sea: noun
know / no	know: verb / no: interjection, adjective, or adverb
counsel / council	counsel: verb / council: noun
pray / prey	pray: verb / prey: noun
profit / prophet	profit: noun / prophet: noun
waist / waste	waist: noun / waste: verb
wave / waive	wave: verb / waive: verb used in legal business
there / their / they're	there: adverb / their: possessive adjective / they're contraction
to / too / two	to: preposition / too: adverb / two: number
pear / pare / pair	pear: noun / pare: verb / pair: noun

List 151 Continued

sent / cent / scent	sent: verb / cent: noun / scent: noun
peek / peak / pique	peek: verb / peak: noun / pique: verb
eye / aye / I	eye: noun / aye: adverb or noun / I: first person singular pronoun
holy / wholly / holey	holy: adjective / wholly: adverb / holey: adjective

ear Reader

I sincerely hope that you have found this book helpful and that it has made the task of teaching English spelling a little less frustrating. If there is anything that you strongly disagree with, please don't hesitate to contact me. If you really like the book and want other teachers or parents to discover it, please consider writing a review on Amazon.com or for your local newspaper. It would be greatly appreciated.

Sincerely,
John Fulford.

64923904R00082

Made in the USA
Middletown, DE
20 February 2018